Are you having problems communicating
  with those you love?
Do your relationships end with anger
  and bitterness?
Are you leaving your life to fate?
Do you find yourself wondering what
  you are doing wrong?

Hilary Rich, author of *HOW TO BE A
GREAT CATCH* shows you in this step-by-step
guide how to make what is wrong in your life
right.

Whether you are coming from a string of broken
relationships with no promise for a future or just
want to lead a happier, healthier, more fulfilling
life with another person—this is a book for
YOU!

HOW TO BE A GREAT CATCH

A Step-by-step Guide
to Attracting the Mate
of Your Dreams

Hilary Rich

AVON BOOKS ◆ NEW YORK

HOW TO BE A GREAT CATCH is an original publication of Avon Books. This work has never before appeared in book form.

AVON BOOKS
A division of
The Hearst Corporation
1350 Avenue of the Americas
New York, New York 10019

Copyright © 1995 by Hilary Rich
Back cover author photo © 1994 Barry Slobin
Published by arrangement with the author
Library of Congress Catalog Card Number: 94-96259
ISBN: 0-380-77841-6

First Avon Books Printing: February 1995

AVON TRADEMARK REG. U.S. PAT. OFF. AND IN OTHER COUNTRIES, MARCA REGISTRADA, HECHO EN U.S.A.

Printed in the U.S.A.

RA   10   9   8   7   6   5   4   3   2   1

To my husband, Steven,
the greatest catch of all

ACKNOWLEDGMENTS

I could not have written this book without the enthusiasm and support of my husband, Steven. He kept distractions out of my way. I feel so lucky and blessed to share my life with someone so wonderful.

I want to thank my very supportive family and a special thanks to my siblings: Dena Samuels, Kirk Citron, Gavriella Aber, and my cousin Todd Berliner for their invaluable assistance on the manuscript. And thank you Dena for all your extra time and effort.

I also wish to thank my students and my readers of *Get Married Now* for their boundless enthusiasm and for asking the questions that sparked the idea for this book.

And thanks to Christine Zika, my editor at Avon Books, for her fanatical dedication to clarity.

And, lastly, I want to thank our two little ones (one on the outside and one on the inside), who kept me company while I wrote this book!

CONTENTS

READ THIS FIRST

Most people live their lives hoping that "someday" everything will turn out the way that they want it to. They keep waiting for fate to turn in their favor or for luck to give them everything they desire. They sit around waiting for someone spectacular to walk into their lives so that they can live happily ever after. What they don't realize is that waiting does not produce results.

The book you are holding will show you exactly how to turn "someday" into today. Rather than wishing and hoping that your life will turn out the way you want it to, this book gives you step-by-step guidelines on how to make it happen *now*. By learning how to be a great catch you are taking control of the one area in your life over which you have the most power: *yourself*. By the time you finish reading this book, you will have more self-confidence than you have ever had. You will have a higher level of self-esteem. You will be the kind of person that you've always envisioned yourself. Your life will begin to look the way that you've always wanted, and you will be more attractive to others than ever.

I want to take you from wherever you are in your life, and bring you to a place where you not only *are* a great catch, but you *feel* like one as well. I want you to have the confidence to go on a date and be able to say, "It's *their* loss!" if you are rejected. I want you to be able to go out with someone who has everything going for him or her and feel *deserving* and *worthy* of that person. I want you to be able to look at yourself in the mirror and smile unabashedly. I want you to be able to appreciate yourself in a way that sparkles and draws others to you like a magnet. I want you to be able to walk into a room with confidence and charm and to feel wonderful about yourself. And most importantly, I want to help you to maximize your own potential so that you can marry the best person possible! We will accomplish all of this and much more in this book.

You Must Be a Great Catch to Marry a Great Catch!

This book will give you step-by-step instructions on *exactly* how to become a *great catch*. You will learn how to get beyond your history and start with a clean slate. How to develop emotional and environmental stability. How to reinterpret your past so as to empower your future. You will learn about strengthening your communication skills, and growing into the kind of person you have always wanted to be. You will learn how to express yourself to potential mates honestly and warmly. You will learn how to have great character traits, how to empower others, and even some etiquette so that you will feel comfortable in any situation. If you already are a great catch, this book will teach you how to present yourself in the best light and how to find someone who truly appreciates all of your wonderful qualities. Most importantly, you will acquire the tools to help you change, grow, and create your own future—tools that you can use for the rest of your life.

The question that I am most frequently asked by students in my Get Married Now!™ seminars, lectures, and programs, as well as from readers of my book, *Get Married Now: The Definitive Guide For Finding and Marrying the Right Mate for You,* is, "Hilary, what can I do to improve my chances of marrying someone fabulous?" The answer is to be fabulous yourself. This book will show you how.

If I could step out of the pages of this book and face you eye to eye, the first thing that I would do is acknowledge you for your willingness to change and to grow. It takes a great deal of courage to take your future into your own hands. But I also want to point something out. There are two reasons that you might be reading this book. One is that you think that something is wrong with you and you want to fix it. And the other is because you are determined to be all that you can be to maximize your own potential. I recommend that you read this book for the second reason. You need to begin empowering yourself starting right now. Only very strong people have the courage to examine themselves to be the best that they can be. So as you read this book, remember that the challenges you are facing are there, not because you need fixing, but because you have the courage and determination to change.

I have written this book with the hope that the insights will provide a framework for you to become the kind of person that you have always wanted to become. In order to maximize the benefits of this book, you can get yourself a little notebook to answer the questions at the end of each chapter. I would also like to thank my students, who so generously shared their stories with me. All their names and details have been altered to preserve their anonymity. I hope that you enjoy the process of going through this book and that you find it very rewarding. May it assist you to *become* a great catch, to *marry* a great catch, and to create a healthy, stable relationship that will last a lifetime!

With warm regards,
Hilary Rich

Part One

EMOTIONAL STABILITY

Many of my students have a great deal of anxiety because they don't feel emotionally stable. They sometimes feel like they can't cope with their problems, and that they don't have control over their own lives. If you consider yourself emotionally stable, this section can serve as a review. But for the rest, who feel powerless over their own moodiness, who struggle with emotional roller-coasters, who depend a great deal on external factors for happiness, and who feel very needy one moment and then push someone away the next, this section will be like water in the desert.

Emotional stability means managing your emotions rather than allowing your emotions to manage you. Can you imagine what it would be like to have your boss scream at you and not have it affect your self-worth? Can you imagine going on a date, really liking the person, and not being devastated when those feelings are not returned? And can you imagine how much you could accomplish if emotional turmoil didn't keep you from performing at your best?

Many of the students from my Get Married Now™

seminars ask me, "My life is a mess, how can I expect someone to want to share it with me?" It is true that the more emotionally stable you are, the more stable a mate you will find, but the process of self-growth begins by first accepting yourself. People need to change to fulfill their potential, not because there is something wrong with them. What makes humans so incredible is their ability to take charge of their own futures. To assess their lives, to plan new directions, and to take action. Your goal is to be a great catch. And you begin by establishing emotional stability, the foundation for a healthy and successful life.

The first step is to get beyond your past. It is important to get over the patterns that prevent you from getting what you want out of life. The second step is to reinterpret your history so that it empowers you rather than drags you down. This is essential for those who feel that a person of quality would never want to marry someone with a sordid past. The third step is to take responsibility for your life. And finally you will learn to master your reactions and maintain stability. By the time you finish this section, you will know how to be emotionally stable!

Get Beyond
the Past

Anne, a student from my Get Married Now™ seminar, said that every time anything bad happened, like her car breaking down or the scale tipping over her usual weight, she had an overwhelming feeling that her whole life was falling apart. She would think about all her past failures and brood over each one of them. Not only did this make the immediate problem unbearable, but it also left her powerless to overcome the particular obstacle in her way. Can you see how her past was following her around like a ball and chain? That is why it is so important to get beyond your past. To forgive yourself for your mistakes. To tell yourself that you did the best you could at the time and next time you'll do better.

Acknowledge the Past

Many people keep their skeletons stuffed so tightly in the closet that they expend all of their energy just keeping that closet door shut. Denial is the sure way to keep them festering in your life. Beth told me that she hadn't had a steady relationship for over eight years. On the telephone, through tears, she told me that she had accidentally become pregnant in her twenties and had had an abortion. Sobbing, she said that she had never told anyone about it, afraid of what they might think about her. For eight years, Beth had lived a life of misery: closed off from other people, closed off from her feelings, and closed off from herself. Because of her denial, she hadn't even allowed herself to mourn her loss.

One way to acknowledge your past is to get a pencil and paper and write down the facts. What happened? Who was there? What did they say? What did they do? When did it happen? Then ask yourself how all this makes you feel. What kinds of feelings have you been holding onto from this incident that have kept you stuck in the past? Examine every major incident in your life, and try to discern how each has affected you. Someone whose parent has died might be insecure in relationships for fear their partner might leave as well. Someone whose parent was abusive might be hostile and abusive toward a future mate. A man whose wife committed adultery might never trust a woman again.

Try to see how past incidents have created ongoing patterns in your life. A pattern is a repeated way of behaving that is a learned response from the past. Most of the time, you follow a pattern without even being aware of it. The very moment you understand what has created a pattern in your life, you gain power over that pattern, and you have a choice as to how you would like to behave from that moment on. If you are having difficulty seeing your own relationship patterns, look at your last few intimate relationships. How did they end? Usually that is a good way to gain insight on your patterns.

Some people have a difficult time communicating.

Others are not able to make a commitment. And some people have a great deal of anger that they are not able to get on the other side of. We form our patterns from role models and certain incidents in our lives, and the better we are able to understand our patterns, the more power we will have in overcoming them. Acknowledging your past and learning from it will keep you from dragging yourself down because of old mistakes.

Forgive Yourself for Being Human

Once you acknowledge your past, remorse will follow. Jack's remorse over his life was written all over his face. He held his head low, his eyebrows looked as if he were apologizing for something, and he spoke without conviction. He told me that he was very interested in getting married, but having been divorced twice, he felt he was just carrying too much baggage for any woman to take. He not only felt bad about how his life had gone so far, but he also felt powerless to do things right for a next time.

You need to take control of your future by taking control of your past! Do you see how Jack is a victim of his past? He needed to forgive himself for being human. He hadn't even given himself the understanding and compassion that he would probably give a friend. He was wallowing in his past and keeping himself from fully living life. When Jack finally forgave himself for his past in the demise of his two marriages and for holding onto the petty anger that drove his wives away, he could finally get down to the business of overcoming his past. Jack and I worked together to learn from his two divorces and find out what would make him a better partner in the future. One of the things we discovered was that he never felt appreciated. He set off a pattern in which he would go out of his way to do things for his wives, and then when they didn't appreciate him to his satisfaction, he would seethe quietly without communicating his dissatisfaction.

We determined that once trust developed in his next relationship, he was going to tell his mate about his pattern. That way both would be prepared if he were to try and sabotage the relationship, and they could discuss it in the hopes of assisting Jack to overcome this obstacle he had set up for himself. In future relationships, Jack is going to try to communicate his feelings rather than hold a grudge against his partner for weeks.

The key here is to realize that we are all victims of our past patterns. Only by recognizing these patterns and forgiving ourselves for being human can we have any power to make peace with our pasts instead of being victims of them for the rest of our lives.

Resolve Your Issues

The next step in getting over your past is to resolve the issues that stand in your way of being close to people. Whether that means that you work these issues out yourself or with others, that is to say, you communicate with the people involved in a past incident, join a support group, or go to a therapist, it is imperative that you leave your past behind. But this will take some effort on your part. Most people are addicted to their dysfunctional patterns. Shelly felt very comfortable in a relationship with a man who was verbally abusive. She was so used to her father's verbal abuse that this unhealthy pattern had a stronger hold in Shelly's life than any notion she may have had about a healthy relationship. When I talked to her about this, she agreed wholeheartedly with me about her pattern, but she is still with the same verbally abusive boyfriend. Seeing the problem is only half the battle; it takes determination to get on the other side of it.

Jim realized that he had a pattern of dating women who treated him poorly. Sometimes women would take advantage by asking him to fix things around their homes, and then they would break up with him. Or women he dated would constantly put him down as if he wasn't good enough for them. Or they would act nicely until they knew he was attached to them, and then they acted like they were only going out with him until they found someone better. When Jim gave his pattern serious thought, he realized that it had first started with his ex-wife. She had been incredible kind and complimentary during their courtship, but the moment they married, she began abusing him verbally. She would criticize everything he did, and always made him feel inadequate.

Since the time this pattern was set in motion, all of Jim's relationships followed the same path. And what was most eye-opening for Jim was the realization that he actually attracted people who would treat him poorly. Their behavior felt familiar, and he found comfort in the familiar.

By understanding the source of his pattern, Jim was able to make a conscious decision only to have relationships with women who would treat him well. He intends to accomplish this by taking the time to get to know someone well before he becomes attached to them, and by constantly being aware of the pattern that predisposes him to find women who treat him poorly.

Resolving your past issues may take time. These patterns have been with you for a long time and can stem from simple repeated incidents or from traumatic events that seem to scar us for life. Anything that has happened to you, no matter how bad, is part of life. You may feel that you are the only person on the planet Earth who has had a tragic event occur, but you are mistaken. The very scars that you feel mar you give you individuality. This may mean that maybe you are more compassionate to others with similar issues, or more able to deal with difficulties than most. They may even be the source of you being the kind of person who would read this book. You are obviously interested in being the best *you* that you can be. You are interested in fulfilling your potential as a human being and as a wife or husband. If you didn't have your particular past, perhaps you wouldn't be interested in self-growth at all.

Once you have understood your patterns by communicating to others and by making the commitment not to let your patterns keep you from getting close to people, it is important to focus on the future. Some people want to stay stuck in the past—in many ways it is more comfortable than having to change—but the process of getting beyond the past is in direct contradiction with your desire to stay the same. Only you have the power to create a new future for yourself. If it helps, every time you become remorseful about the past, say to yourself, "I have a clean slate and can create my own future!" Only persistent effort and determination will result in old patterns falling away, allowing you to create new relationships based on more healthy, stable patterns.

NOTEBOOK

- What incidents from the past still haunt you?

- For each incident, write down the facts: What happened, who was there, what did they say, what did they do, when did it happen?

- For each incident, write down how you felt at the time.

- How does the fear that a mate will find out about these incidents affect your relationship? (Examples: fear of loss, lack of intimacy, etc. . . .)

- How do your relationships usually end? (A good indicator of your relationship pattern)

- What do you intend to do to make sure that your past does not interfere with your future relationships?

Reinterpret Your History

Here are two interpretations of the same event: Jill's parents divorced when she was thirteen. Her father made many promises to visit her, but he always broke his promises. He also promised her gifts he never gave and vacations he never took with her. As a result, Jill has a difficult time trusting people. In every relationship she holds back intimacy for fear that the men will make promises that they won't keep. She has low self-esteem and difficulty relaxing because she is afraid to lose control of a situation.

Okay, second interpretation: Jill's parents divorced when she was thirteen and after that her father made many promises he did not keep. Upset, hurt, and angry, Jill talked to her mother, who helped her understand her emotions. As a grown woman, Jill has a great deal of compassion for others who have also had splits in their family. She also has a high level of self-reliance, and since she feels she could survive anything, she's not afraid to take risks in life.

Both these interpretations may be true, but the question is: Which interpretation leaves Jill weak and a victim of circumstances and which gives Jill power in her life?

Examine Your Interpretations

You have the power to interpret your past in any way that you want. If you say your mother was emotionally abusive to you and that's why you have a hard time relating to people, you do not have the power to change your ability to relate to people. Whereas, if you say she was emotionally abusive, and therefore you are more sensitive to other people's feelings, you are creating an interpretation that makes you stronger and gives you more power. In the example, the first Jill is someone in need of consoling, the second Jill is someone who would climb to the top of a mountain! Can you see how the interpretation of the past makes the first Jill emotionally unstable, and the second Jill strong and steady?

It is important to recognize that you aren't reinventing the past. You aren't covering up the facts. You are just interpreting the facts in a way that empowers you. Take a look at your life. How have you interpreted your past in ways that have left you powerless? What interpretations keep you stuck in the past? How can you reinterpret the past to empower you in the future? The power of this process is that it changes your history from *dysfunctional* to *experienced*.

You would think that Cassandra had all the reason in the world to have a difficult time with men. Her father was an alcoholic and had left her mother four times before Cassandra was ten years old. Audrey sat next to Cassandra in my seminar. The two of them were partners in an exercise and they shared their results with the group. Audrey's father had also been an alcoholic, and she had a lot of pent-up anger. But Cassandra wasn't angry at all. What the two of them realized was that Cassandra had something that Audrey didn't have: the opportunity to resolve the emotional turmoil her circumstances had created. Cassandra's older sister had acted as a buffer and a support system, someone Cassandra could talk to so that she could approach her situation without feeling victimized. She learned from her sister that it is not what happens to you that counts, but how you take your circumstances and turn them into advantages. Cassandra spent her late teens working at a youth center and became the confidant to many kids who were going through similar difficulties. From this she gained a sense of self-worth and value. Cassandra said that if it weren't for her history, she would never be the person that she is today, nor would she be as helpful to others in her career as a social worker.

On the other hand, Audrey's interpretation that she was the victim of her father's abuse left her powerless. Her interpretation kept her anger in place, and as a result she lashed out at the men in her life. Cassandra agreed to meet with Audrey and help her recognize how the anger toward her father was costing her her happiness. Examining the way we interpret our histories is a powerful step toward empowering our futures.

Create New Interpretations

Take a pad and pen and write down a particular incident in your life. Then write down your current interpretation of that incident. For example, your father never picked you up from your piano lessons on time. Your current interpretation might be that your father never cared enough and thus behaved irresponsibly when it came to your welfare. Now, on the same pad write down a new interpretation that will be empowering to you. For example, you could write that due to your father's negligence, you learned to be more responsible.

Angela told me that her past was so awful that no reinterpretation could possibly work. She hated men because one night when she had drunk too much at a college party, a man took her up to her room and raped her. She said that there was no excuse for what he had done, he was a horrible human being and deserved the death penalty. She wished she had prosecuted him at the time, but she had been too embarrassed. Angela's anger is certainly well founded. She has a right to be angry. But to hold this incident against all men for the rest of her life is an awfully big price to pay.

Perhaps Angela needs counseling, but maybe she could also create a new interpretation of the incident that would allow her to at least begin the healing process. I suggested several possible interpretations. I suggested that the incident might have taught her to be more compassionate to others who have been victims of violent crimes, or that she might be a better mother in terms of teaching her children self-defense techniques, or that she might even start a rape-crisis hotline. Whatever her new interpretation, there is absolutely nothing Angela can do to change history. Her only chance of getting beyond this incident is to work through the emotional trauma, and to create a new interpretation that will empower her.

In other cases, it is helpful to regard difficult incidents as integral parts of our growth. Someone may say, "You know, if I hadn't been fired from my job, I would never have started my own business," even though at that time he may have been devastated by the job loss. But by creating a new interpretation, he is empowered by a once-horrible incident.

Practice Your New History

Reinterpreting your history only counts if you can make it empower you. After Audrey received coaching from Cassandra for her past regarding her alcoholic father, Audrey looked past her anger and resentment and looked at her father from a different angle: as a man unable to express his love for his family. Controlled by his drinking, he felt unworthy and so he would spend a lot of time out with his friends. But it was his love for his wife and children that made him stay in the marriage and make repeated attempts to give up his drinking. Audrey realized that it was her father who did not have self-worth, not she. As a result of this reinterpretation, Audrey learned that communication is the cornerstone of every relationship. This new interpretation gave her the strength and determination to become a brilliant communicator.

She called up her sister and talked about their childhood, saying that it is important the two of them bury old wounds in order to move on in their lives. Her sister, still in denial, did not want to discuss the past, so Audrey called her older brother. The two of them commiserated for hours, and Audrey told him how important it is to communicate in a relationship. Her brother agreed and added, "It is amazing that you could say that after all we've been through." Audrey told me that they had never had such an intimate conversation in their whole lives.

By practicing her new interpretation, instead of being weakened by her past and feeling undeserving of a quality mate, Audrey now feels that she has strength of character and the ability to make the best of a situation—which makes her a great catch in anyone's book! But it is important to realize that many people carry their "baggage" around like trophies. In a sense they are attached to their pasts. They have "victim syndrome," and use it to get sympathy from friends and partners. They spend their lives acting out patterns that give them no power over their lives.

Your new interpretation will be a stabilizing force in your life. And though you will likely have minor setbacks along the way, don't get discouraged, just review your new interpretation and start again. The habit of blaming your past for your problems will disappear soon, and in its place will be emotional stability.

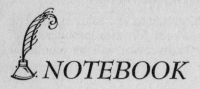

NOTEBOOK

- What circumstances in your life make you feel victimized?

- What interpretations do you have of your past that are not empowering to you?

- What kind of traits might you have developed because of your interpretations?

- Write down a particularly traumatic incident in your life: who, what, when, and where.

- Write down your current interpretation of that incident.

- Now write down a new interpretation that will be empowering to you.

Take Responsibility
for Your Life

A few years ago, I worked on a volunteer project with a woman named Janice, who was a member of my committee. She was a very warm person and fun to be around. However, each time I asked her to do something, she would call me up with a reason why she didn't do what she had promised. The first time her three-year-old was sick, the next time her husband's car broke down, and then the repair man never showed up. After many weeks, I finally told her that I wanted results, not reasons. This prompted her to give me more reasons for her inability to accomplish her duties. I finally stopped asking her to do things, and then she complained that she wasn't being included in any of the plans!

Janice never acknowledged that she had broken her agreement to accomplish a task. Instead she placed the blame elsewhere. It was as if she were mere dust in the wind, subject to whichever way the wind was blowing at the time. But you and I know better. If we really want to get something done, we get it done. We aren't so powerless that we have no control over our environment. And regardless of whatever obstacles may come your way, a little ingenuity can go a long way when you are committed to accomplishing your goals.

When her three-year-old was sick, Janice could have asked a friend to pick up the copies from the printer. When her husband's car broke down, she could have made those phone calls from the pay phone at the mechanic's. When the repairman didn't come, she could have left the house anyway to keep her agreement and reschedule to get her dishwasher repaired another time. With determination, she could have kept her commitments. Obviously, when push came to shove, circumstances got the best of her.

You may have been raised not to take responsibility for your actions. You may have had role models who spent a lot of energy placing blame elsewhere rather than producing results, too. But being responsible means being in control. And the most powerful way to be emotionally stable is to take responsibility for your life.

Stop Placing Blame Elsewhere

The first step in taking responsibility for your life is to stop placing blame elsewhere. That means that the buck stops with you. To be a mature adult is to keep your commitments when you make them and not to spend your life making excuses otherwise. You are responsible for anything that doesn't work in your life. It is your responsibility to handle whatever obstacles and circumstances come your way. Many people walk around with chips on their shoulders, as if life has done them wrong. And maybe life has been hard, but placing the blame on external factors leaves them powerless to do anything about it. They are stuck being victims. On the other hand, if they were to say, "These are the cards I've been dealt, how can I make the best of them?" they would have the tools to control any situation.

Consider a family where the father is at the mercy of his company. His boss demands one hundred and fifty percent, and the father delivers. This, of course, is at the expense of his wife and family. He gets home after the kids are in bed, and his wife gets to spend two hours with an exhausted grouch. This man tells his wife that he must work such late hours in order to provide for the family. This man deserves a great deal of credit for working hard and doing what he thinks is best for his family.

Now, take another man, also totally committed to his family, who recognizes that he is ultimately responsible for the quality of his life. He also works very long hours, but he decides he wants to be with his family more. He marches in to his boss and tells him, "Listen, I love this company. You know I work very hard for you. But as a family man yourself, you can understand that young children need their father. I am committed to making this company number one in this city, but it cannot come at the expense of my family life. I am willing to work all day, two hundred percent, I'll even skip lunch if I have to, but at six o'clock, I go home." With this tactic, he may lose his job or he may not. But in any case, he is taking responsibility for how his life will go. Rather than going home, complaining and blaming his boss for making his life miserable, he is taking the bull by the horns and making his life work.

Stop Complaining

Many people complain because they feel someone has done them wrong. They feel that they are owed something. They may be perfectly justified in their assessment of the situation, but complaining robs them of all of their power. Allowing every situation to victimize you makes it easier to abdicate responsibility for the circumstances of your life. This is very natural, even if it is neither productive nor satisfying. It takes a very mature individual to look for solutions, not blame.

Several years ago, I met a woman named Julie who was in her twenties. Her mother had died when she was young, and as the eldest daughter, she had helped raise three younger siblings. The remarkable thing about Julie was that she was not bitter about the loss of her childhood, nor that she had to help support the family instead of going to college. Julie's view was that everything that happens teaches you a lesson about life.

For instance, when Julie had her car stolen, along with her favorite leather jacket and a box of cassette tapes, Bonny, Julie's co-worker, had to drive twenty minutes out of her way to drive Julie to work and back. After four days, the car was recovered. There was a rip in the backseat and all of her possessions were missing. She shared this thought with me: "I had become very attached to my possessions. When they were stolen, it made me realize that life is too short to focus so much attention on material things. Also, spending so much time commuting with Bonny made me realize that I was really missing close friendships in my life. This incident made me see that I should focus more on creating friendships and put less energy on acquiring things."

Every time the opportunity to complain arises, you have the choice about what to think, what to say, and what to do. But first, you need to recognize each time you are complaining and for what reasons.

Picture this: A man drives up to a woman's house for their first date. She greets him at the door. He tells her that her dress is pretty. She says, "They didn't press it right." He opens the car door for her, both get in, and he turns on the radio. She says, "There are no good radio stations anymore." They get to the restaurant. They order and when the food comes she makes a sour face and says, "It must be a new chef." Doesn't it sound like an enchanted evening? Do you think this man would consider her for marriage?

Complainers may want to keep people at a distance, or it may be that they want others to feel sorry for them or they seek attention. Whatever the source, some people seem to enjoy complaining, but after a while, no one listens. People are not attracted to people who complain all the time. You need to decide if the benefits of complaining outweigh the costs.

Complaining gives you the chance to let off steam, lets you impress others by accurately criticizing something, gives you the satisfaction of knowing you are right, and gains your friends' sympathy. But by the same token you can wear out the patience of those who must listen to you. You lose power over a situation because you are seen as a victim, or your friends tire of consoling you all the time so that when you really do need them, they aren't there for you. If you consider the consequences of your habitual complaining, you can correct your habit if you choose to do so.

Stop Criticizing

Criticism has its place in terms of analyzing things to determine where improvements can be made, but all too often it is used to put people or things down. Some people criticize as a way to make themselves seem better. If you point out how sloppily someone is dressed, doesn't it make you feel better than them?

Greg is a brilliant lawyer. He is one of the best litigation attorneys in the city. His phone rings off the hook and he lectures to many organizations. He came to my course because he wanted to find the obstacle in his way of finding a mate. Well it didn't take us long to find it. Whenever anyone raised a hand, Greg would quickly challenge him or her in the most aggressive manner. Obviously, Greg's training had taught him to be very critical, but in his social life he had not learned to remove himself from the courtroom. What Greg came to realize was that he would pick apart his girlfriends until they couldn't bear it. Criticism tore his relationships apart. His addiction to winning an argument and his skills in proving how right he was left him successful and very alone. He learned that he had to listen to another person without jumping in with his critical opinion. Recognizing this pattern will be a major step for Greg in terms of developing relationships with others.

Still others feel the world owes them something, and they complain about not getting what is rightfully theirs. Such as, "It's not fair that plumbers make so much money, I work just as hard as they do." Or, "Government employees get off on holidays I have never even heard of. I should too!" Or, "My brother got a loan from my parents, I should get one too." Rather than focusing on how the world is treating you, maybe the focus should be on how you treat the world. Part of taking responsibility for your life is to focus your attention away from yourself.

Often people think "who wants to be concerned about others when those people are probably only concerned with themselves anyway? Why should I care about them?" The reason is that people who focus on others live happier, more satisfying lives. And, most importantly for emotional stability, focusing on others stops you from obsessing about yourself. You can stop wondering what is wrong with you, what you should be doing, and what others are thinking about you! What a relief and pleasure to let go of these concerns! The way to get rid of them is to concentrate on assisting others! Learning to be that kind of person takes time, but anyone can accomplish it with persistence.

Complaining is also unhealthy for a relationship. Many people feel that complaining is just a way of communicating, but it's not. For the most part, complaining is destructive whereas communication is constructive. Complaining is a one-way street. The complainer doesn't take the other person into account. It is almost as if the person complaining is a tape recorder with the play button on, not even caring about the listener's opinion. Communication, on the other hand, is a two-way street. The communicator judges the mood of the other person before speaking, then he/she listens carefully to what the other person says. The communicator truly cares what is going on with his/her partner.

The effects of complaining and communication are also different. Complaining pushes someone away, whereas communication draws someone closer. The reasons why someone would want to push another away vary. Maybe one is stuck in a pattern of pushing someone away in order to then reconcile and get closer. Maybe one feels uncomfortable being close so he/she complains to keep a partner at a distance. Now that you know that your complaining pushes someone, a potential mate, away, you can stop your complaint mid-sentence and attempt to communicate instead.

Barb is an outgoing person who enjoys having many planned social activities. However, her boyfriend is much more of a loner, and this difference has caused difficulties in their relationship. So Barb has taken to complaining to get what she wants from her boyfriend, regardless of his needs. When she wants to go out with friends, go to the movies, or rent videos, complaining gets her needs met. She says, "You never take me to the movies," so he takes her. Or, "Every time someone invites us out you say we can't go and I am sick of it!" So her boyfriend takes her to the party even though he doesn't want to be there. The problem is that Barb and her boyfriend do not have healthy communication. Barb's boyfriend resents her demands. And Barb has turned into a whiny person. This situation is a time bomb waiting to explode. Barb needs to work on her ability to communicate her needs. Instead of complaining, she should sit down with her boyfriend and come up with a solution. They might decide to go out once a week only. Or they might figure out which social activity he dislikes the least. Whatever the compromise, both should be happy with the resolution.

A pattern of complaining will persist until a better alternative is created. Communication is the best way to overcome complaining, but first you must recognize the cost of complaining to your relationships, your stability, and your control over your life. Becoming a noncomplaining person is well worth its own rewards. Don't take my word for it. Just once, when you start complaining, stop yourself. You will be amazed at the sense of strength you feel within yourself. The less you complain, the stronger you will feel. Complaining casts a gray cloud over everything so that things seem worse than they really are. You will notice that a complainer's life does look miserable. Then you will be able to look at your own life and count your blessings.

Stop Being Self-Absorbed

Taking responsibility for your life means to stop being self-absorbed. In a society that places personal happiness above all other goals, this poses quite a challenge. When we were children deciding whether to be ballerinas or firemen, we were told, "You can do anything you want as long as it makes you happy." As struggling teenagers we were told, "You can't please everybody so you might as well please yourself." As adults, we go by the adage, "You better look out for number one." This focus on personal happiness has a price—a price to families, a price to communities, and a price to the world. Imagine what it would be like if people focused on others rather than on themselves. Instead of everyone clamoring to gratify themselves, everyone would likely get most of their needs met by others giving of themselves.

Think about the emotionally stable people you know. Aren't they usually interested in what is going on with you? They don't dump all of their problems on others either. Of course they have problems, they're just not absorbed in them. Deborah is a very nice person and very in touch with herself. But when you have a conversation with her, she details her latest discovery about why her life doesn't work. I keep pushing her to do some kind of volunteer work in the community. I can't think of anything else that will get her mind off of herself.

Brad needed to have all his material comforts. He worked hard to buy a condo, a sports car, and a boat. Similarly, he considered his girlfriends as material objects, and there to provide only for him. He came to one of my Get Married Now™ seminars because, although he had everything, he could not find a woman with whom to have a meaningful relationship. He sorrowfully admitted that women were only interested in his money. They did not care about him. In fact, Brad realized that he did not care much about them either. What we worked on in the seminar was how Brad's whole life revolved around himself. He spent every ounce of his energy working on acquiring material possessions to satisfy his needs. He never put any energy into getting close to others. Realizing this, Brad has made a commitment to himself to spend more time asking others about their lives. Not only to get his focus off of himself, but more importantly, he will now be able to get closer to others.

Taking responsibility for your life means focusing on the world revolving around you, recognizing when you are self-absorbed, and stopping yourself mid-sentence and asking the other person about themselves. Groucho Marx had a great line. It goes, "Okay, enough about me. Let's talk about you. What do you think about me?" Part of being a person of quality is that there is more to your life than yourself. We will be exploring ways to connect with people in later chapters, but for now, practice asking people about themselves, and you will be astonished at how your relationships and your life improve.

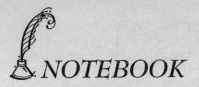

NOTEBOOK

- What aspect of your life have you been blaming on someone or something else?

- What do you complain about?

- What alternative to your pattern of complaining can you create?

- Are you self-absorbed?

- What actions can you take to turn your focus towards others?

Master Your Reactions

Melinda sat in the front row of my Get Married Now™ seminar. She wore a neat suit with a string of pearls, and had a handsome leather notepad on which she took notes. She always asked appropriate questions, and returned on time from each break. But I noticed that every time I would bring up the subject of interdependence versus independence in marriage, she would recoil. Finally, I called on her to speak her mind. She said that she had worked very hard to be successful and to gain her independence, and she would never give that up. So I told her that I understood how she felt, but that in turn she would have to give up her desire to be married. A lengthy battle ensued. My contention that marriage does not consist of two independent persons, but of interdependence, was very upsetting to her. What we soon realized was that at the heart of this issue, Melinda had an enormous emotional stake in her ability to be independent. She watched how dependent her mother was on her father, and she never wanted to be in a submissive position like that. Whether or not Melinda was right or wrong, this emotion permeated every aspect of her life, even to the point of getting in the way of her relationships. Identifying her reaction, and the power that it had over her, was the first step toward overcoming its role in her life.

Identify Your Reactions

Before mastering your reactions you must first identify them as they happen. Every emotion that you feel will elicit a reaction from you. If someone yells at you, you may react by pouting or yelling back. If you feel jealous, you may react with pettiness. If you feel hurt, you may react with anger. Mastering your reactions means that you decide how you want to act, rather than just reacting reflexively to the outside stimulus. For instance, if someone cuts you off on the freeway, your immediate reaction might be anger, so you honk your horn for five minutes to let them know just how angry you are, or you speed up to the other car and shake a fist at the person. Some people might even react with fear, pulling off the freeway to get over their fright. But in all of these cases, people's reactions are automatic, with no thinking process involved. There was no choice in how they reacted.

Having mastery over your reactions means that when something occurs that causes you to have a particular emotional response, you take a deep breath and think before you react. Let's say your boss tells you that you must work late. Your typical reaction might be to complain to her that you worked late three times last week. This time, however, you stop and think. What would be the most productive way to handle this? You decide that complaining has never succeeded in lessening the workload. How about suggesting that you go in early the next morning instead, or that you eat lunch while working at your desk for a few days? The point is to think before you react.

Identifying your reactions is the first step toward having power over your actions. It is very valuable and healthy in a relationship to identify your anger, and then to exercise your self-control over it. Anger can cause irreparable damage, and you cannot apologize or take back words said in anger. Indulging oneself in outbursts of emotion causes pain and instability in a relationship. It would be much more powerful to get over the angry emotions, and to handle the situation appropriately.

I saw an amazing example of self-restraint in the supermarket. A woman had a toddler in her shopping cart as well as a young child of about six who was busy exploring the aisles. The mother kept reminding him not to touch anything, but more than once she had to rescue items from falling. I could see that trying to get her shopping done while watching the toddler and the young boy was wearing her patience thin. Finally, the boy accidentally pulled a stack of tissues down. I was prepared to see a major reprimand. When I brought my cart into their aisle, I witnessed what had to be an extremely angry woman carefully handing each box of tissues to the young boy as he piled them back on the shelf. When they were through, she knelt down and looked him in the eye. I couldn't hear everything they said, but I heard him say he was sorry. For the rest of the shopping trip, the boy behaved perfectly.

When I consider this woman's patience, I am awed. Think about the consequences if she had reacted with anger. She would have screamed at the boy, making him feel very bad, making herself feel bad, ruining their shopping trip, and most importantly, she would have lost the precious opportunity to be a role model for her child. I am certain that the reason the boy behaved so well for the remainder of the trip was that he modeled his mother's incredible restraint. He knew that his mother must have been extremely agitated, and the fact that she handled it so well and kindly taught him how to act kindly and well toward her.

There is a theory that says when you feel anger, you should express it or else you will get an ulcer. But maybe it's not holding onto the anger that is the problem, maybe it's withholding communication that causes resentment to build. If you can learn to share your feelings, not only will you be happier with yourself, but you will be a better catch for someone. Obviously the woman in the supermarket knew how to communicate effectively with her son. Expressing anger can cause irreparable damage in a relationship. There is always a better solution. You need to find it.

Being emotionally stable means experiencing the vast range of human emotions, but not dramatizing them to the point of absurdity. Being a great catch means mastering your reactions so that people can relate well to you, can understand you, and can be close to you. People actually repel others by indulging themselves in emotional tantrums. You can control your reactions to any emotion.

Of course, we all have strong emotions, that's what makes us passionate in our lives. But weird, irrational behavior does not engender love and caring in the people around us. People want to have some sort of predictability and consistency in their relationships to make them feel stable and secure.

Vanessa was always the life of every party. Everyone invited her because she was wild, sassy, and very funny. She was thoroughly enthusiastic about life and was determined to try everything. She went through boyfriends like other people go through shampoo. Her emotions ran hot and cold. One moment she was totally attached to you, and then she would instigate a horrible fight. In two years she had had four different jobs because of "personality conflicts." Without getting into all of the psychological reasons as to why Vanessa might be like this, think about the following questions. Would Vanessa be the kind of person you would invite to a cookout? Would you want her to be your defense attorney? Would you want to have to count on her to support your family financially? Would you want her as a role model for your children?

Someone looking for a marriage partner wants stability. Many of my female students say they have met men who seem to be people of quality, but they find them boring. The first sign of a stable, healthy, dependable, predictable person is that at first they seem very boring! They seem boring because many women consider wild, passionate men attractive. All too often these men will offer some exciting times for a few months, but the fire soon dies. A man who is consistent and dependable may not buy you an extravagent gift or dance with you all through the night, but you can count on him to call you after a nice evening together, or be supportive when you are feeling low, or help you clean your garage.

People who master their reactions may indeed seem boring compared to someone ranting or exposing his feelings blatantly. But if you take a closer look, you will notice that they are also more mature, emotionally healthier, more stable, and all in all, great lifetime partners. Everyone is searching for peace and serenity, but the very moment they find it, they interpret it as boring!

Practice Stability

Sometimes we are so used to the way we do things that it seems absolutely impossible to do them any other way. So to get used to being an emotionally stable person, practice being stable. The ideal way to do this is to find a role model who is a stable person. Try to imitate their reactions. Try to think about what this rational person would do in a similar circumstance. Try to think about your own reactions and how they differ from their reactions. Your objective is to act stable as a way to strengthen your stability muscles. Don't be concerned if you slip often at first. Acting irrationally and emotionally just means that you are still in the process of learning. Just remain determined to make ongoing, steady progress toward being stable.

It is also important to stop creating ghosts. Many of my students, well into their thirties, are convinced something is wrong with them. They feel that they are emotionally unfit for marriage, that they have too much baggage, that they have destructive patterns that will keep them from ever getting married. They need to stop worrying. Everyone feels this way at some time. Yet, ninety-five percent of all people get married, and seventy percent of all divorced or widowed people get remarried. So stop worrying! You have many strengths and many weaknesses, just like everyone else on the planet. You are even more remarkable in that you are working to make the best of your strengths and improve your weaknesses by reading this book. Just focus on behaving in a stable, dependable manner. Don't allow yourself to get rattled easily, and think before you act.

Handle Bad Times Well

Mastering your reactions also means handling daily crises as well as bigger tragedies and stressful periods in your life with as much aplomb as possible. It's not that emotionally stable people don't have downswings, it's just that they handle them better. Rather than avoid thinking about bad times in the hopes that they will never materialize, it is far more useful to plan how you will handle them when they do come. Bad times come in three levels of severity: being upset, being in a bad mood, and being depressed.

It is important to recognize that when many people feel upset they use it as an excuse to treat people poorly. Mastering your reactions means that when you are upset, you don't take your frustration out on others. Whether that is someone in your family or the grocery store clerk, emotionally stable people don't give themselves permission to make someone feel bad. It's amazing how treating someone well when you are feeling bad mysteriously makes you feel better too! Sometimes being kind to someone while letting them know that actually you are pretty upset about something else is quite astonishing to them. You can actually inspire them to better handle their own moods.

People are usually upset by something that goes wrong in their daily routines, or by another who may have intentionally or unintentionally harmed them. When you are upset try to discern what the cause is and what about a particular situation has upset you, then discuss the details with a friend. This is the most effective way to get over being upset.

Dierdra said that she would find herself upset several times during the day. We soon discovered that she had a short fuse, and got frustrated easily. I asked for an example of the last time she was very upset. She said that last week she had lost the last eight pages of a report by not saving them on her computer before she turned the machine off. She went home from work feeling like a complete failure, and angry that she would now have to turn the report in late. She remembered part of the lost report, but reconstructing it was going to be difficult and cumbersome.

Dierdra kept rethinking about shutting the computer off, and the empty feeling she felt a moment afterward when she realized the pages were lost. She was making herself sick over it and hardly slept at all that night. Instead she should have called a friend as soon as she got home and discussed her feelings of frustration and anger. It is important to find friends who listen to the ups and downs of your daily life. Dierdra also could have made a one-page outline of those lost eight pages to present along with the first part of the report so that she would have felt better going into work the next morning. And finally, she could have altered her perspective on the loss. Dierdra could have said to herself that the new eight pages she was going to recreate would have been ten times better than the ones she lost!

A bad mood is usually the result of a general feeling of discontent. But there are many ways to handle your moods well if you prepare for them. It is important to remember that everyone has mood swings, so you shouldn't think that there is something wrong with you. You just need to learn ways to make them easier on yourself, and easier on others. The first thing to remember is that it is a bad mood, not a bad life! Often, in the midst of a bad mood, it certainly feels like your whole life is falling apart. Avoid the natural tendency to count all your troubles. While brooding, people often talk themselves into frenzies, which makes them feel worse, and definitely makes it harder for them to get out of their bad moods. On the other hand, you can talk yourself out of your mood. By recognizing a bad mood, telling yourself that it is only a temporary condition, and making a list of all of the good things about your life, you can replace that frown with a smile in no time.

Instead of being grouchy around the house, or snapping at everyone, acknowledge aloud, to yourself and to others, that you are in a bad mood. It will give your mood less power over you. And your admittance makes you less inclined to be hostile. Communication has an amazing way of making you feel that you're not alone. Calling a friend to let her know you're in a bad mood is helpful, too. Try this the next time you're in a bad mood. You'll be surprised at how much better you'll feel afterwards.

Bad moods are like the weather. They seem to come and go when they feel like it, and it really isn't even necessary to analyze why you are in a bad mood. It may be for no reason at all, and spending time trying to figure out who did something to harm you, or what is wrong with your life that is putting you in a bad mood, often makes you wallow in the mood. It is much more useful to discover what things get you out of a bad mood. Every time my friend Laura gets in a bad mood, she puts on an old Beatles record and eats a bowl of mint chocolate-chip ice cream. Some people go shopping, others find that writing down a list of things to do gets their minds off themselves. Visiting a friend or relative in a nursing home, or doing something for others often helps snap you out of your mood. You can also act as if you are in a good mood in the hope that it will grow on you. Most importantly, remember to treat others nicely while you are in a bad mood. This will make you a more thoughtful, caring person.

Depression occurs when you don't feel good about life for an extended period of time. During this time, it becomes difficult to focus on anything else but your own troubles, and it seems as if this overwhelming feeling will never end. It is hard at this time to focus on being a great catch. Mostly you just want to sulk. This is a time when you don't want to be so hard on yourself. Many people seek the assistance of a trained therapist during these times to help them get through lasting periods of depression. But for any type of depression, short or long, there are five things that you can do to make that time easier.

Number one is to get as much sun as possible. I cannot stress this enough! Sunlight works miracles for depression. Second, have three balanced meals every day. When people are depressed, either they eat all day long, or they don't eat at all. Three balanced meals help make a person feel well balanced, physically and mentally. The third thing is to exercise as regularly as you can. Exercise tends to shorten depression time, and researchers are not even sure why! Fourth, wake up early. Sleeping till eleven increases the depth and duration of depression. Finally, sleep for an extended period during the night. Taking daytime naps and sleeping off and on during the night prolongs depression. Try to get all of your sleep at one time during the nighttime. These pointers should assist you in getting through your depression, but be sure to contact a therapist or doctor if your depression continues for a long time.

Jan spent a few days sulking in bed during her menstrual cycle each month. She feared that if her future mate knew about this, he would think he was marrying someone who was mentally ill. I had another student who was very depressed because he had lost his job. He refused to look for a wife until he was employed again. I told both of these students that it's not what your circumstances are, it is how you handle them that makes the difference. Rather than feeling bad for herself, Jan should accept her monthly mood and realize that it doesn't mean something is wrong with her. And rather than putting his whole life on hold and feeling terrible about himself, my student should recognize that being unemployed is a part of life. Emotionally stable people seem to have internal reserves that act as a buffer through rough times. They have an underlying sense that the future will be okay. Remember, it is not what happens to you during your life that matters, it is what you do with it: how you handle it, how you learn from it, and most importantly, how you handle others during it.

NOTEBOOK

- What extreme reaction (ie., anger, fear, hostility, jealousy) do you have and how do you usually react when you have this emotion?

- Who can be your role model of a stable person to help you practice acting stable?

- What do you usually do when you are upset about something and what can you do that might be more productive?

- What do you usually do when you are in a bad mood and what might you do that would be more productive?

- What actions can you take to be better prepared to handle bad times well?

Maintain Stability

Don't judge whether you have achieved emotional stability by how you feel at a particular point in time. Day-to-day life has so many ups and downs that you may not always *feel* stable. Stability can only be judged by looking at your life over the course of time. Just do your best to maintain stability each day, and the weeks and months will take care of themselves. Every time life throws you a curve ball, get right back up to bat. The following guidelines will assist you in maintaining emotional stability.

Think Things Through Thoroughly

Every time you are about to make a decision or need to solve a problem, think to yourself, "I better use the four T's." The four T's are: Thinking Things Through Thoroughly. It means asking yourself three questions: What results do I want to achieve? How do I plan to accomplish these results? What obstacles might get in my way? By thinking about these three questions, you are better prepared to make the best decisions possible. You will be much more emotion-

41

ally stable, and you will feel calmer, more at ease, more in control, and you'll be able to enjoy your life more.

The first question, "What results do I want to achieve?" needs some serious consideration. I had a woman in my Get Married Now™ seminar who kept arguing with everything I said. When I said that you should find out as much about a person as possible on the first date, she said that doing so took away all the fun. When I said that you should ask your partner if they planned to get married in the future, she said that the question killed spontaneity. But the bottom line is, if your goal is *marriage*, then these questions I suggested are vital to ask on the first date in order to find out as much as possible about the other person. You must know your partner's intentions or you may spend a lot of time with someone who will not marry you in the end. The point is that determining what results you want to achieve is an incredibly valuable tool for creating your future.

The second question you should ask yourself is, "How do I plan to accomplish these results?" It takes creativity and brainstorming to come up with solutions to problems, especially when they have to do with our personal lives. Many business people have no problem creating brilliant plans when it comes to work, but they don't use these same skills in their own lives. Jeff was not very happy with his relationships with women. He always seemed to find women that he couldn't fully trust. He went from one relationship to another, and when the women were ready to make commitments, he would break off the relationships. He was not cruel, he just didn't make getting married a priority in his life. This had gone on for close to eight years. Given that Jeff was a successful attorney who assisted many companies in developing their business plans, it was almost shocking that he never developed his own life plan. Most people don't stop to consider what they want in their lives and how they plan to attain their wants once they have thought them out. What Jeff needed to do was determine what he wanted to accomplish. He was not happy with his current situation, but he never sat down to figure out exactly what he wanted either. During our lengthy discussions, Jeff reluctantly admitted that he had a hard time trusting women and if he found someone he could trust, he would want to get married.

The next step was for Jeff to determine how to accomplish this. We decided that a short course of therapy might be valuable to overcome his fear of trusting. This was not easy for him, but he was truly committed to overcoming whatever obstacles stood in his way in order to accomplish his mission. The next part of his plan was to join a matchmaking service so that he could learn a little bit about each date before he went out with them, which would serve to lessen his fears. And the third part of his plan was to talk to the women he dated about his difficulty with trusting others so that maybe they would be better prepared to support him. Jeff did an excellent job of planning, and you can see how he has much more power now over his future by having thought things through thoroughly.

The third question, "What obstacles might get in my way?" is easiest to answer. You simply make a list of possible obstacles on a piece of paper. For Jeff, the list of obstacles in the way of his getting married included a busy work schedule, avoiding confrontational therapy sessions, finding a woman indifferent to the whole issue, and fear of resorting to his old patterns rather than working on what he truly wanted in his life. Making a list of obstacles not only helps you prepare for them, but when they occur, they have much less power over you and become much easier to overcome.

Thinking things through thoroughly is one of the most valuable tools for making decisions about your future, but it is also a great method for responding to stressful situations in your life. If your boss unexpectedly sets an appointment to see you, instead of being anxious all day, thinking it through will empower you to be at your best when you walk into her office. Think about what she may want. Is there anything that she could be upset about? Make a few lists: Are there any new projects that she might assign to you? What is the best thing that can happen? What is the worst that can happen? By preparing, you can strengthen your ability to act powerfully.

It is important to consider all of the possible outcomes of a decision. Think about what might happen if you take a particular course of action, or what results might occur if you take an alternative course of action. Think about what could possibly occur that you don't expect, what turn of events might occur that will change a situation completely, what could go wrong, and what is the worst thing that could happen. Rather than worry about what might happen, plan ways to overcome any obstacles. By thinking seriously about the future, you give yourself an optimal chance to handle a situation masterfully.

Of course, you can become obsessive thinking about the future, and this can be a mistake also. Set aside a certain amount of time to think about a particular issue, do the best you can within that parameter, and then move on to something else. Once the time is completed, follow your plan of action and stop worrying about it. You have thought it through thoroughly. You can stop worrying because you have done the best that you can.

I noticed that many of my students seem to do everything in their power to avoid looking at the future. Maybe they don't want to take responsibility for it, maybe they don't want to ruin the surprise of the unexpected, maybe they are too busy to think about it, but one thing is certain, if they don't manage their futures, their futures will manage them.

Feeling more in control of your future sure goes a long way toward making you feel more emotionally stable. It reduces the anxiety about what is in store for you. Of course, much of life cannot be planned or expected. But thinking things through thoroughly gives you a definitive advantage in managing your life, and managing the unexpected.

Beverly is a very practical person. She is the administrative assistant to the vice president of a large bank. She keeps her desk organized, drives an efficient car, and keeps in shape by eating well and working out a few times every week. But when it comes to her personal life, she plays it all "by ear." She does not want to plan her own future because it is far too exciting to be surprised by what might happen around the next corner. The only trouble is, no matter how many corners she's turned, she has not yet found what she wants out of life. So far she's been in four long-term relationships, none of which have resulted in marriage. And it is marriage she's looking for. She's never been to Europe, but she buys travel magazines all the time hoping one day she'll eventually get there. And she bought a home computer because she hopes to one day write a novel. Beverly has many dreams, but never makes any concrete plans to carry her dreams out.

Beverly attended my Get Married Now™ seminar because her best friend forced her. She was one of the most reluctant students I've ever had. The problem was that Beverly didn't like the idea of making a plan to find a mate. She wanted to depend on fate and romance to find the man of her dreams. It wasn't until we had spent several hours discussing the issues of romance that Beverly came to see that romance never got her what she really wanted. She wanted to get married to a man who was totally committed to his family, someone who had integrity, loyalty, and good communications skills. By gaining clarity on what she needed to be happy (values, not romance), she realized that she would have more power over her selection if she took action rather than if she let fate take care of it for her! She had to take the reins and manage her own life to get what she wanted rather than wait for it to come to her.

Thinking things through thoroughly gave Beverly the answers she needed. She determined that she was going to get married within the year, that she would go with her new husband to Europe on their honeymoon, and that she would write the outline to her novel within three months. Beverly was not the same person she had been before she made this statement. Everyone in the seminar room was inspired by Beverly's boldness! And Beverly even looked different! Her look of resignation was replaced by determination, and there seemed to be much more of a lightness in her manner. But the most important thing is that Beverly is on a new course in her life, and she is the ship's captain.

Be Consistent

People have no idea how powerful it is to be consistent. You can often accomplish more by being consistent than you can by being bold. The first key to being consistent is not to make promises you can't keep. Don't tell someone you will write them a letter every week unless you can do it. Don't tell your boss you can finish the report in a week unless you have done it before. Don't promise your friend that you will paint her whole apartment in one day unless you know you can realistically accomplish this.

Being consistent means making your best effort to do what you say. Many times people can't do what they say because they have promised someone the moon. It is okay to have lofty goals, and to aspire to great things, but what you promise someone is a different story. Only promise something that you are confident you can deliver. Consistently keeping your promises is difficult even when they are simple, manageable promises. But by making outrageous promises, not only do you damage your ability to accomplish what you've promised, but if you don't do what you promised, you damage your credibility with others, and worse yet, with yourself.

Janice decided to volunteer at a fund-raiser for a local charity. Overly enthusiastic, she promised the committee that she would triple the amount raised from the prior year for the upcoming charity dinner. Even under the best of circumstances, this would have been close to impossible. And unfortunately, Janice had to compete with another charity banquet that was held on the same night. Janice would have been much better off if she had made a private goal for herself of doubling the funds raised. That would have been more attainable, and she would still be considered consistent and credible by the committee. You want to be enthusiastic about your goals, but at the same time remember that consistency is the backbone of accomplishment. Consistency means committing to something for the long haul rather than for the big splash. And consistency is a great quality to have to be a great catch!

Consistency also means not making excuses. That people can count on you. Try your best to do what you promise, but when you can't, don't make excuses. People who often give excuses act as if it is never their fault that they were unable to fulfill their word. If you can't keep a promise, simply apologize and take responsibility for it without blaming some external reason. We all know people who never do what they say, and have a million reasons for each instance. Don't you get tired of listening to their lame excuses? Taking responsibility for keeping your promises not only builds stable relationships, but also makes you feel good about yourself.

Consistency also means not quitting. The first thing we usually want to do when times are rough is to drop all our obligations and hibernate. This is perfectly natural, but the problem is that the moment we stop fulfilling our obligations, we stop feeling good about ourselves and about our lives. Many people use the excuse of going through difficult times as a way to avoid being responsible. People become so preoccupied with themselves that they don't consider the consequences of their actions, which is why when things are tough, it is especially important to keep our promises and commitments. Not only so that others can depend on us, but even more importantly, so we can depend on ourselves.

Every time Rebecca went through a breakup in a relationship, she would go for several weeks without cleaning her apartment. She would be so depressed that she just didn't feel up to keeping it clean. And the more time that passed, the more onerous the task became. Obviously coming home from work to a disaster area did not help her sad mental state. In fact, it made it worse. In the roughest times, it is especially important to be consistent with the day-to-day caretaking of our lives.

Communicate Fully

Communication can solve almost every one of life's ills. As long as you can talk about something, it can be made better. In times of instability, sharing your feelings can relieve some of the burden. In times of great joy, telling others about your happiness can increase your fulfillment. Communicating with others is the best asset you can have in managing your relationships and your emotional stability.

It is vital to make a commitment to communicate fully with your partner. That means that if either of you feels the necessity to discuss something, the other person can't ignore the situation. He or she is obligated to discuss it. In many relationships, people all too often let things slip under the rug, or they just don't feel like exerting the effort of fully disclosing their innermost thoughts. And sometimes they don't feel like listening to what their partner has to say. This can lead to a buildup of resentment and misunderstandings. Communication isn't just a nice idea in a relationship. Communication *is* the relationship. Making the commitment to communicate fully ensures that you and your partner will always be there supporting each other.

If you have a sink of dirty dishes, and you pile on one more dish, you probably won't notice it until it becomes too ugly to look at or until the stack tips over. However, if you have a perfectly spotless sink, and you put one dirty dish in it, it would really stand out. It's the same way with communication. With every withheld thought or angry feeling that is not verbalized, it is like the dirty dishes piling in the sink. These feelings won't disappear by themselves, and unless you discuss them with your partner, just like the pile of dishes, the resentment and anger will build until your relationship breaks apart. Discussing the issues that affect your relationship is how you keep your "sink" clean.

Here are a few tips about communicating fully. The expression, "never go to bed angry" is important for a happy marriage. So is finding the time to communicate, such as at dinner time, right before going to sleep, or even on the phone during the day. It is also important to forgive each other for the inevitable things that happen between two people who are very close and to make agreements about how to handle difficult times.

Vickie had just broken up with Ed three weeks before she came to my class. She said that there were many things that didn't work in the relationship. Ed was often irritable after work, and he took it out on her. He was also inconsiderate, often arriving an hour late to pick her up. Ed also put her down constantly. When I asked Vickie about Ed's response to these issues, she looked at me inquisitively and said that she had never discussed them with him. What surprised me was that Vickie and Ed had been seeing each other exclusively for two years. What had they been doing for two years?

If Ed was irritable after work, maybe he didn't realize it. If Vickie had brought it to his attention, he probably would have made the effort to change. Maybe the two of them could have brainstormed ways Ed could overcome his after-work frustrations. If Ed arrived late, Vickie could have told him that this upset her and refuse to go out with him if he arrived late again. Maybe when Ed put Vickie down she could let him know that it bothered her. The point is that without communication, there is no relationship. There is just two people reacting to each other. Relationships aren't easy. They take work. And that work is communication. With solid communication, a solid relationship can provide the most satisfaction and fulfillment in your life.

While examining your communication skills, you should consider what stops you from communicating fully. Consider how you related to past partners and with members of your family. If your family tended to suppress its feelings, then you might suppress yours. If there was a great deal of anger present on a daily basis, you will likely express this same anger. Your past relationships created your patterns of communication. It is very important to examine these patterns and to determine how your communicative ability might be improved.

Whenever there is a problem, Mark's girlfriend Deborah has to practically squeeze his feelings out of him. He will pout for hours waiting for her to ask him what is wrong. Then he will reluctantly respond, but he will have no idea what is upsetting him. Their conversations usually last hours, and not only does Deborah find it frustrating, she also finds it hard to feel close to him. They have been going out for four months, but Deborah already is getting tired of his inability to communicate his feelings. The problem is that Mark has a pattern that stops him from communicating fully. Mark grew up with three older siblings who dominated his household as a child. Mark was lucky if he ever got a word in edgewise at the dinner table. So now, as an adult, Mark tends to hold on to his feelings and talk only when necessary.

This problem can be solved if Mark can recognize the source of his pattern, and work toward overcoming it. He needs to recognize that pouting is his way of controlling the situation. He needs to learn how to discern what upsets him, and how to express himself verbally. He needs to overcome his destructive communication patterns and create a closeness to Deborah. And most importantly, he needs to commit to the project of being a good communicator—a goal which will inevitably prove invaluable in all aspects of his life.

A great catch also knows how to communicate in a healthy way. People are not born to be naturally good communicators. It is a skill that needs to be learned. Most people do not make good communication a priority in their lives because they assume that if they can talk they can communicate. Unfortunately, that's not true. Communicating is when you express a coherent thought, the other person understands what you mean, and they respond in the same way. This is harder than it sounds. Often it is difficult to understand our feelings, so talking about them is even harder and sometimes the other person isn't in the right frame of mind to hear what we have to say. We can't always assume that the other person understands us, our feelings, or the situation. Sometimes there isn't adequate time to convey all of the subtleties we would like. But if you make every effort to share your thoughts with your partner, pay attention to whether they have understood you, and listen carefully to what they have to say, you will be well on your way to being a great communicator and a great catch!

It is also important to realize that every word you utter has a profound effect on other people. Many times people become angry and don't stop to consider the effects of their words. Angry words can leave long-lasting scars. It is fine to express your anger, but there is no need to be melodramatic. Choosing your words carefully is often more effective in getting what you want anyway. If you yell at someone, they may give you what you want, but they will resent you and won't be so inclined to give in the next time. It never pays to fight dirty. It might feel good at the time, but you will always end up paying for it one way or another. You might damage a close and loving relationship or the other person may lash out by being verbally brutal as well. Watch your tongue before you say something you'll regret. Leave the room if you need to calm down and think. Your strength during those times will give you the greatest gift you could ever have—closeness and trust with one another.

And if you do say something in anger, apologize as soon as possible. The longer you wait, the harder it will get. Even if you feel as if you are the only one apologizing, do it anyway. It is not worth risking your closeness to a loved one. And your own emotional stability depends on it. Being emotionally stable isn't based on whether you have problems or not, it's based on how well you handle the problems that come up. Apologizing quickly is one of the sure signs of someone who is more committed to a successful relationship than to being "right."

Many times I have been asked, "Shouldn't a husband and wife tell each other everything?" The definitive answer is "No." Many people think that they are communicating fully because they say whatever is on their minds. Saying whatever is on your mind is not being communicative, it is being irresponsible.

You need to choose your thoughts carefully. Think about what you really want to say. Don't tell your husband that your old boyfriend was a better driver. That will only make him feel bad. If you talk to a friend about your relationship with your spouse, don't tell your spouse that your friend agrees with you about an argument the two of you had. That will only embarrass him or her. Communication is at the heart of all of your relationships, and it needs to be handled delicately.

Developing the art of diplomacy will take you a long way. Instead of saying, "Take out the trash," you might try saying, "It looks like the trash pail is full." Subtle, yes, bossy, no. And give up pouting. Yes, it can be very attention-getting, but take responsibility for yourself instead. Communicate what needs to get said and stop burdening people with having to dig information out of you. And if someone is sensitive about a particular subject, don't talk about it. Of all the ways to maintain emotional stability, communication is the most powerful. And it is within your power to be a great communicator.

In this section you have learned how to get beyond your past, to get over the patterns that prevent you from getting what you want out of life. You have reinterpreted your history so that it empowers you rather than drags you down. You have learned how to take responsibility for your life. And you have learned how to master your reactions. Finally, you have learned the importance of maintaining emotional stability. You now know how to manage your emotions! And you are on the road to being a great catch and to having a much happier, healthier life!

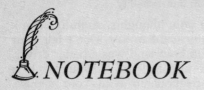

NOTEBOOK

- What area of your life have you been leaving to fate that you would now be willing to take control of?

- What actions will you take to produce the results that you want to achieve?

- What promises have you made in the past that you were unable to keep?

- What can you do to be more consistent in your life?

- What kinds of excuses do you make when you don't do what you promised?

- How do you react when your life gets difficult? What might be a more productive response?

- What stops you from fully committing to something?

- In what ways could you improve your communication skills?

Part Two

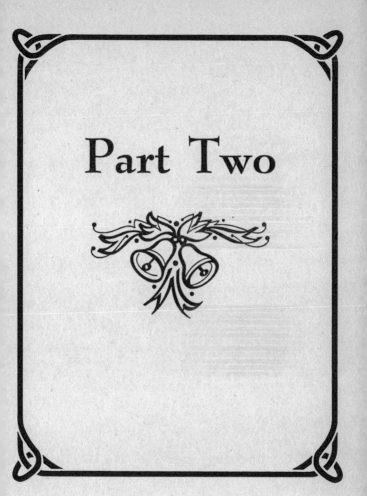

Part Two

ENVIRONMENTAL STABILITY

After the work that you have done on your emotional stability in Part I of this book, the best way to ensure that you maintain emotional stability is to create a stable environment around you. A stable environment will also make you a happier person, and a great catch for marriage! As you progress through Part II of this book, acknowledge yourself for the parts of your environment that are already stable, but be strong enough to recognize the parts of your environment that are not. Only by taking a hard look at your situation will you be able to have the power to change it.

Do you have a history of changing jobs, going from one relationship to another, and moving around a lot? Examine which of these situations might pertain to you: You don't have a workable relationship with your family, you don't have friends that you can depend on, you are unable to hold down a job for more than a few months, you have been evicted by your roommate for not paying bills on time, your social circle changes radically and frequently, you don't have a support system in your life, you don't have any hobbies, or you aren't involved in community activities. Scrutinize your own life to determine which of these areas you need to work on.

A chain is only as strong as its weakest link, and the same is true for your environment. If you have a great family life, but you can't hold down a job, your whole environment suffers. Your life will not be balanced and the problems caused by your inability to keep a job will affect all other areas of your life. You will also have difficulty maintaining your emotional stability because of the turmoil that is created by this problem. That is why it is so important to work on all aspects of our environment simultaneously. Each area does not have to be perfect, but we must continually strengthen our weakest links at the same time that we enhance our strongest ones.

There are five areas to consider when creating a stable environment. First, you need to come to terms with your family. Many people would rather ignore their parents and siblings and try to make a clean start. Unfortunately, we are all victims of our family patterns. The first chapter will give you in-depth assistance in getting beyond these specific patterns in order to have a great relationship with your family. The second step is to attain great friendships. Friends are life's gift, and not enough people know how to be a good friend. The third step is to develop stability in your career. This is an area wherein many of my students feel much anxiety. This section gives you guidance on exactly which areas to focus to make your job as stable as possible. The fourth step is to learn how to create a community that makes life much more fulfilling. And the fifth step is to find a hobby, one that will interest you, and in turn make you more interesting! By the time you finish reading this section, you will know exactly how to create a stable environment in your life, which will help you to reach your fullest potential as a human being.

Family

The very word *family* conjures up images of hearth and home. Of Mom and Dad surrounded by kids. Of laughter and noise on a sunny day. Grandparents sitting on the couch and a dog lying under the coffee table. The only problem with this picture is that it's someone else's family! So many of my students in my Get Married Now™ seminars tell me that they come from "dysfunctional" families. Many feel as if they will never be able to create a stable family of their own. Family patterns are indelibly fixed upon our psyches. Whatever doesn't work in your present family relationships will haunt you in all other relationships. Just because we ignore them does not mean that they do not exist. And the best way to plan for a stable family of your own is by first resolving old issues involving your parents and siblings. This might be bad news to those of you who have a great deal of anger and resentment towards your family, but without fixing the past you cannot cast the foundation for a stable and happy life in the future.

Discover Your Family Patterns

Before creating a great relationship with your family, you need to discover your family patterns. Every family has its problems. Some are severe, and some more average may seem dysfunctional because people's expectations are so high. Some people measure their families against fantasy families they have seen on television. But you must realize that no one's life is ideal. We are dealt certain cards, and it is up to us to make the best of them. For better or worse, our family environment has played a major role in making us into who we are today. Now, it is up to us to make the most of it.

Jeffrey had a problem with his mother. He told me that although he loved her very much, he needed to move across the country to get away from her smothering ways. Yet, she still intruded in his daily affairs. She seemed to go out of her way to annoy him. If she called at night and he wasn't home, she would call back every hour and leave anxious messages. When Jeffrey arrived home and listened to them, he would be so furious that he wouldn't even call her back. Of course she'd then call at two in the morning to make sure he was safe. At thirty-four years of age, this was unbearable for Jeff. As a result of this pattern, Jeffrey would only date women who made no demands on him, and let him come and go as he pleased. But in a healthy, stable relationship, it is *essential* that two people are able to make demands of each other. That is part of being a team, and the way two people develop trust for one another. Jeffrey's family pattern was interfering with his ability to have a healthy relationship with a partner.

A good way to discover your family patterns is to write them down. This will help you look at things more clearly. It will also help you focus your energy on a few problematic areas rather than feeling as if the whole family structure doesn't work. Think about what most annoys or frustrates you about a relative's behavior. You might start with each of your parents, and then go through each of your siblings. Write down what you feel doesn't work in each relationship, and what you feel are the areas most needing improvement.

In Jeffrey's case, he wrote down: Mom constantly interferes in my life. This was a good start, but he would be more effective correcting this problem if he were more specific. He then added: She calls me too often, asks too many questions about my personal affairs, sends me too many clothes, stays too long on visits, bugs me about getting married. The beauty of writing all this down was that when Jeff was finished, he looked as if he had a huge weight lifted off his shoulders. Plus, when I asked him if there was anything else that bothered him, he said, "No." How powerful! Having it all down on paper made this major problem in his life seem surmountable!

Jeffrey wrote down similar lists for each of his two sisters, and even a list for his father, who had passed away. His father's list included: He never gave me the approval I wanted, got way too angry about stupid issues, didn't have his priorities straight in terms of spending time with us, and didn't give my sisters as much freedom as he gave me as a teenager. Jeff was able to tackle these issues with his father by writing him a letter and resolving them, at least in his own head. Right now, write down all of *your* family patterns in your notebook.

Next, write down how you wish things could be. Jeff wrote: I wish my mother would stop calling me so often, I wish she would wait for me to tell her what's going on in my life rather than hounding me for details, I wish she would come for shorter visits, and I wish I was able to talk to her about these issues without her getting defensive and upset. This exercise is valuable in that it allows you to visualize what it would be like if these patterns were overcome. It also gives you the opportunity to let go of some of the issues that haunt you. Sometimes we can't see how things could possibly improve until we visualize them and think about ways to make things better. Continue in your notebook and write down how you wish things could be.

Examine *your* role in how some of these destructive patterns continue. We are not always victims of these patterns; sometimes there is a benefit for us to keep them going, otherwise we would not let them persist. Many times people would rather be right than happy and some are actually addicted to making others "wrong." Still some people feel powerful by withholding intimacy, or abdicating responsibility.

Jenny had a very stressful relationship with her mother. They talked on the phone often, but they were constantly battling over everything. If her mother said that she liked a dress that Jenny's sister wore, Jenny would say she didn't like it. If her mother disliked Jenny's brother's girlfriend, Jenny would say she liked her. It was almost comical to hear them speak, but this was certainly no laughing matter.

Jenny needs to examine her need to make her mother "wrong." Jenny wrote down that she continued this pattern because she didn't want to give her mother the satisfaction and approval that her mother wanted. It annoyed Jenny that her mother needed her daughter's agreement on her opinions to validate them. Jenny resented being put in this position. By denying her mother this approval, Jenny felt more powerful than her mother. Turn to your notebook and write down the benefits that you derive from your patterns.

Establish New Lines of Communication

With a clear view of your family patterns you are halfway toward overcoming them. By establishing new lines of communication, you are creating a structure for interrelating that works. It will be almost as if you are creating new relationships with the people you have known your whole life.

Begin by discussing the difficult issues in your family relations. You can use your notebook as a guide, but remember, your objective is to overcome destructive patterns, not to make your family feel bad for everything that's wrong in your life. You have to be willing to take responsibility for the patterns, and to acknowledge your role in maintaining these patterns.

Nadine had a pattern of ignoring her father's advice. In every conversation, she would tell him what was going on in her life, and he would give his opinion on the matter. She would get annoyed, but she would continue to recount all the details of her life, and rebuff him every time he interfered. Nadine discovered that she found satisfaction in rebuffing her father. She felt he was always trying to dominate the situation, and this was her way of rebelling.

Nadine sat down with her father in the hopes of overcoming the pattern and improving her relationship with him. If she had started off the conversation by complaining that he always tries to dominate the situation, even though it might be true, you can easily see that he would put up his defenses and their discussion would get nowhere. Instead, Nadine told her father that she recognized that when he gave her advice, she often rebuffed him. She apologized to him and said that only recently did she recognize her actions. She also told him her reasons. Her father's reaction was more positive than she expected. He acknowledged that he could be very opinionated at times, and often recognized that he pushed his opinions on her, but he couldn't stop himself. He took the blame for always trying to dominate a situation. He also told Nadine that he hoped she understood it was not his desire to be right that made him behave this way, but his love for her and his greater desire not to see her hurt. As Nadine and her father fully discussed this issue that had become an obstacle in their relationship, and as both took responsibility for their roles, a new line of communication opened between them.

Once you establish new lines of communication, learn to apologize, forgive, and then move on. This part of the process allows you to clean the slate. Developing a stable relationship with your family is everyone's secret dream, but many people don't want to take the time and effort to make this happen. Often they are addicted to set ways and don't wish to attempt something that will disrupt the ways they know and are comfortable with, even though they may not be healthy. Sometimes dysfunctional patterns are so ingrained in our systems that only with the help of a trained therapist can these patterns be overcome. But if you are determined to have a great relationship with your family, all obstacles can be overcome.

Betsy didn't call her mother very often because her mother always put her down. She criticized everything Betsy did. Betsy decided to call her mother and confront her about this problem. She told her mother that the reason she didn't call more often was because she was tired of being criticized. Betsy's mother denied these accusations, and in fact became very angry. The call ended with her mother slamming down the phone.

Two days later, Betsy called her mother again. She apologized for putting her mother on the defensive, but said that the two of them had to work this issue out or it would continue to interfere with their relationship. This time Betsy's mother agreed to listen to her. Betsy listed many criticisms that her mother had made to her, and then she said, ''I am not trying to make you feel bad, I am just trying to get you to see things from my side. I feel that until you see how you put me down, you will continue to hurt me with your criticism."

Her mother didn't say very much during that conversation, but the next day she called Betsy and told her that she was sorry for all of the times she put her down. The two of them then established new lines of communication with each other: They made an agreement with each other that if Betsy's mother puts Betsy down, Betsy would say, "Mom, you're criticizing me," and Betsy's mother would acknowledge it and start her sentence over again. Making this agreement was a powerful step toward building a strong, healthy relationship. It will also create a bond of trust between Betsy and her mother. She will no longer be in constant fear of her mother putting her down so she will be more comfortable calling her mother more often. This in turn will make her mother happy.

Create Methods for Resolving Conflicts

Every relationship has conflicts. They are part of life, and often offer valuable ways for us to learn about one another. What differentiates stable, healthy relationships from unhealthy ones is not whether there are conflicts but how well those conflicts are handled.

In creating strong relationships with your family, you must find methods for resolving whatever conflicts may arise. Often people don't consciously consider how they will handle conflicts, they just react without thinking. Their patterns determine their behavior, not their minds. Your objective is to develop productive methods for resolving conflicts. This will not only assist you in strengthening your family ties, it will also establish a foundation that will assist you in developing closer relationships with every person in your life.

Megan's mother constantly tells her to improve

herself. She tells Megan to wear more attractive clothing, to cut her unruly hair, and to eat more politely. Megan responds by wearing the most unattractive outfits she can find, keeping her hair unkempt, and being quite casual in the way she eats her food. This pattern has been going on for over sixteen years.

Megan and her mom sound like two broken records every time they talk to each other—and unfortunately there is no communication between them. With time, this pattern will intensify when more serious issues come into play. At some point Megan's mom will push her daughter to marry a respectable husband and Megan, in turn, will probably find some man who is just the opposite. Megan's mom will never achieve her real desire in life: To see her daughter get the most out of life. And Megan will never allow herself the freedom to choose what she wants out of life either, as she is always basing her rebellious decisions on how they will spite her mother.

Once Megan discovered this pattern, and the cost associated with it, she had several heart-to-heart discussions with her mother. She acknowledged her rebelliousness, but also pointed out that her mother constantly imposed her will. They analyzed the pattern from all sides, both taking responsibility for their roles, and forgiving each other for the hurts they'd caused over the years. They aligned on a common goal to fully communicate any time this issue resurfaced. This communication process is not easy and takes time, but ultimately Megan and her mother should be incredibly proud of their efforts.

But it's important to realize that conflicts never cease to arise. As soon as they had come to a truce, Megan's mom called and told her daughter that her rebellious streak may be interfering in her other relationships and that she should really work on controlling it. Regardless of how true this may be, Megan's mother has just taken one step back in their relationship. Information offered of oneself should not be used against that person. And it is essential that you plan ways to resolve such conflicts if they arise.

Conflicts are much easier to resolve if you are prepared for them. Instead of reacting with anger and surprise, take the time *before* a conflict arises to brainstorm how you will handle it. Think about what conflicts might arise in your relationship. Together, make a list of these possible conflict scenarios, and then make a list of possible ways for the two of you to deal with them. When your list of solutions is complete, agree on which solution the two of you think would be the most effective.

For instance, one possible conflict that Megan might have with her mom is that she might still feel compelled to tell Megan what to do. Or, as we saw, her mom might use Megan's admittance of rebelliousness against her. Or she might still impose her opinions on Megan, but just approach it more subtly. Or, Megan might have no tolerance for any input her mother might give to her. Maybe Megan will still rebel, but blame her mom completely, forgetting that she is also responsible. Or maybe, over time, they will forget their common goal of full communication. Discussing and making a list of these possible conflict scenarios gives you power over them because you will be prepared.

When making a list of possible solutions to these conflict scenarios, Megan and her mom decided on several solutions. If the conflict is that Megan's mom uses Megan's rebelliousness against her, the two agreed that Megan would say, "Mom, you promised you wouldn't do that." Or they would hang up the phone, redial, and start the conversation over again. They should make the list very long so that they think of as many ways to resolve the conflict as possible, and then they should choose the solution that they both feel would be most effective.

They should choose a solution that won't make

either of them defensive, or either of them angry, that won't make them hold a grudge, and that hopefully adds a level of humor or warmth to an otherwise difficult situation. Your objective is to get on the other side of a conflict with both of you feeling closer. And the beauty of creating methods for resolving conflicts is that you are developing the pattern of working out conflicts together, which is extraordinarily valuable for long-term stability.

Outlining all of the possible conflict scenarios, brainstorming solutions together, and agreeing on a solution takes a lot of time. But remember, you are building the prototype for a powerful, stable relationship. Many of my students have always wanted to know what it would take to have great relationships with their parents. I have just shown you how, but you must be willing to do the work to make it happen. Creating a great relationship with your family through this process helps you to create powerful relationships in all areas of your life, especially with your future spouse.

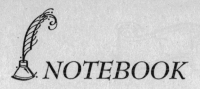

NOTEBOOK

- What family issues annoy or frustrate you?

- How long have these issues been bothering you and how do you plan to solve them now?

- How do you perpetuate some of the destructive patterns in your family?

- Make a list of each pattern that you need to discuss with your family. Then write down the date by which you plan to have resolved a particular conflict.

- What possible conflicts might arise from a situation you consider resolved?

Friends

If you think back to your childhood, besides memories of your family, you probably most remember time spent with your friends. As we get older, and more people come in and out of our lives, we see friendships in a more transitory light. We may not have seen our high school buddies for years, or spoken to our best friend from college since we graduated, and that person from our first job, to whom we confided all our secrets, moved out of town and we lost touch. If you think about it, it seems we are meant to just enjoy each relationship for as long as it lasts.

But think again. Your environmental stability depends on your friendships almost as much as it does on your family relationships. Friends can make life much more enjoyable, by helping us cope during difficult times, making us understand life, by showing us a different perspective, and by helping us maintain our stable environments. Many people think that they can carry life's burdens alone. They claim they are "independent" and can manage everything by themselves. But when the rough times hit, they say,

"Why doesn't anyone understand me?" Someone
would have understood, if they had only reached out
for some help. Other people surround themselves
with many friends who are not supportive and they
suffer as a consequence. This chapter is designed to
help you to create great friendships and to teach you
how to be a good friend.

Discover Your Friendship Patterns

Write down a list of your close friends. Don't include acquaintances. An acquaintance is someone
with whom you have a relationship because of certain circumstances in your life. A friend is someone
who remains your friend no matter how your life
changes. Family members should not be included in
this list. With family members, the permanence of
the relationship automatically creates a level of commitment that must be created in a friendship.

Now take a good look at the list. How does it
make you feel? Are you glad that you have so many
people in your life, or sad that there are so few? Try
to identify an overall emotion associated with your
friends. Try to see what pattern most of your friendships have in common. Do your friends make you
angry? Sad? Happy? Cared for? Rejected? Are your
friends dependable? Do they support you when things
are going poorly? Are they your greatest fans, or are
they the first ones to point out all of your shortcom-
ings? You should find a general trend associated with
all of your friends. Knowing this friendship pattern
will help you develop stable, healthy, satisfying
relationships.

Sarah had many friends, but there were three in
particular that she considered her closest. Amy was
her best friend during her childhood, almost like a
sister. Vickie had been her college roommate for
three years, and Barb was someone she met at her
sports club. When she began looking for her friend-

ship pattern, the first thing that Sarah noticed was that her three friends had one thing in common: All three were undependable. They didn't call when they said they would, they would never stick to any plans they would make, and they relied on Sarah to make all the decisions concerning anything they did together. This angered Sarah and made her frustrated with the three women she cared for very much. When she looked at the other friendship patterns in her life, she noticed that many of her other friends behaved this way as well. Hence, Sarah came to the conclusion that people, in general, are undependable.

Maybe Sarah should examine why she chose undependable friends. What benefit did she derive? There is always a benefit for us when we persist in doing the same thing over and over. In Sarah's case, we discovered that she chose undependable friends so that they would look up to her as the dependable half of the relationship. When comparing herself to her friends, Sarah felt good about how well she handled responsibility. Sarah also noted that since her childhood buddy, Amy, had been dependent on Sarah, Sarah unconsciously modeled her future friendships in the same way. Whenever she met a friend, Sarah would take care of all the decision making and planning. In fact, when she thought back to her college roommate, Vickie, she realized Vickie had actually been quite dependable their first year together. She recognized that Vickie had become more and more undependable with her as the years passed. Sarah saw that clearly she had played a role in creating a relationship with Vickie that fit her friendship pattern, a pattern that caused constant angst in their relationship. Once Sarah recognized this pattern she gained the power to overcome it.

Bonnie told me that in her friendships she always gave more than her friends. She was the one who always initiated getting together, who called, and who did favors without asking for any in return. The emotion she associated with her friendships was hurt at being unappreciated. When Bonnie thought about why she chose the friends she did, it became obvious and she also admitted that a part of her derived satisfaction from playing the martyr, but she didn't know why.

Make New Friends

Given the power old patterns have, some of my students say that they really don't see much future for their current friendships. The relationships are unsatisfying, and not worth the effort it would take to change them. This may be so. It is important to see an objective picture of your friends in order to know how you would like to grow in terms of having satisfying friendships. You may actually drift away from some of your old friends. But whether you create new friendships with the friends you already have, or make new friends, your objective should be to acquire the kinds of friends that you can keep for the rest of your life. Lifelong friendships are a sign of an emotionally well-balanced, stable person.

To make new friends, you must be friendly. This is much easier said than done. Many people go through life so caught up in their own worries that they don't take the time to pay attention to other people. An acquaintance at work might be very upset that her boyfriend broke up with her. Instead of just saying you're sorry and getting back to work, you could ask her out to lunch to console her. This act of friendliness might be the start of a good friendship. Or say a couple from your apartment building asks you to collect their mail while they are on vacation. Instead of grudgingly taking on this "chore," you could use it as an opportunity to make friends. You could ask to see photos of their holiday when they get back. You could even offer to water their plants while they are away. In turn they might invite you to a party or introduce you to someone who they feel would be just right for a friendly person like you.

Making new friends takes effort but it is certainly worth it! Not only for the joy you will attain by having good friends to share your life with, but also because when you focus on other people and their needs, you stop obsessing about yourself. And obsessing about yourself is one of the primary sources of unhappiness. Try this simple exercise: Next time you catch yourself feeling anxious about everything in your life, think to yourself, "Focus on others!" Help an elderly woman who dropped her prescription in the drug store. Compliment a shopkeeper on her dress. Or telephone your sister, brother, or friend and find out what is going on in his or her life. You will find that your worries about yourself will decrease tenfold.

There is a predominant feeling in our society that one must be covetous of one's time and energy as it is thought to be in limited supply. But this is not true. Those that know the secret of being generous know that the more you give of yourself, the more you get in return. Pam is very vivacious and fun to be with in social settings. But when it comes to the office, she lets the pressure of her job affect her personality. She becomes very serious, and is often so engrossed in her work that she doesn't pay any attention to anyone around her. Sometimes she doesn't even respond when someone greets her in the hallway. Pam has gained the reputation of being a hard-nosed businesswoman who would step on anyone on her way up the corporate ladder. People avoid her, and when she has an important deadline, no one gives her any support. The tragedy here is that Pam is truly a nice, caring person, but no one gives her the benefit of the doubt. Because of her lack of friendliness, everyone assumes she is a shark.

Being friendly means going out of your way to be

kind to people. It means saying "Good morning" to everyone at the office, pouring someone else a cup of coffee, or holding the elevator door for someone. It means asking customers if you can be of any further assistance, asking co-workers if they need help, and not snapping at people when you are under a lot of stress. And friendliness means being nice to people who may not have been nice to you, or listening to someone's problems even though you know that they won't listen to your advice afterwards. Friendliness is the quality of being nice in all situations. Of going out of your way to make others feel good. It is one of the shining qualities of a great catch. Everyone wants to be with someone who is kind to others.

A giving person spreads himself or herself in many directions. You can support charitable organizations. Instead of buying another suit for yourself, you take a friend out for dinner. Remember people's birthdays and send them thoughtful gifts. Offer your guests a soft drink the minute they set foot in your house. Give a friend a sweater that you don't ever wear. Let your friend stay over when they need to, even if it is inconvenient for you. Don't worry so much that you might get taken advantage of when you have paid for the movies twice in a row. Give someone an enormous tip for doing a great job. Let someone cut ahead of you in line at the bank. Park your car and pick someone up at the door rather than honking loudly. Stop your car and let someone else pull out of his/her driveway. Spend an extra ten minutes at the bookstore with a friend, rather than pulling him/her away because you are ready to leave.

You have the choice to be giving many times during each day. Giving will not only make you a better person and a better friend, it will make your life less stressful. And do not let your generosity be undermined if someone doesn't appreciate it. What goes around comes around, and by being giving, you *will* have a better life—guaranteed.

As a good friend you must also know how to reciprocate. You must notice when somebody is making an effort to be your friend. If someone calls you often and you are never the one to call first, your friendship won't be able to withstand the imbalance. Relationships work when both people are committed to them, and commitment is only seen through actions. If you are in a relationship where your friend makes most of the effort, you need to take action to balance things. For instance, if your friend initiates most of your outings together, you can offer to pick her up and choose the restaurant. Or maybe your friend always calls when you are sick to see how you're feeling; you should then make the effort to visit her the next time she's not feeling well. If your friend drove you to the mechanic to pick up your car, then you should pay for the gas. Reciprocal actions in a friendship keep it healthy, and are an ideal practice for a balanced, healthy marriage.

A word of caution: There is no such thing as a platonic relationship. It is almost impossible to have a man and a woman interact without some sexual tension present. Even if you aren't sexually attracted to the other person, the tension is still there. Furthermore, they may be sexually attracted to you even if you don't feel the same way. Many students tell me, "But Hilary, we're just friends." But there is no such thing as "just friends." If you are truly serious about getting married you have to examine all of the opposite-sex relationships in your life and how they may interfere with your ability to find a mate. Opposite-sex relationships fill a certain part of your emotional needs that should be reserved for your future spouse. Also, when a potential partner sees you with these "friends" they are less likely to approach you. And, when you do end up getting married, these opposite-sex relationships might interfere with your marriage. My recommendation to you is to spend less effort on your friends of the opposite sex, or even consider ending these relationships.

Make Your Friends Happy

Nothing ever seems as important as what we are going through. You've had a busy day, you're worried about your job, you don't fit into your jeans, and your car needs to be repaired. The last thing you have energy for is to be concerned about somebody else's job, car, or problems. Yet, when someone else phones you to ask how your job is going, whether you had your car repaired, and how the party was last weekend, you certainly appreciate the thoughtfulness. Not only do you feel fortunate to be able to share your life with someone, you also feel a closeness to this person because he/she cares.

You can make your friends happy by showing interest in their lives. This is difficult for some people. Brad confided to me that with his schedule, he didn't have time to make close friends. He liked to go to the gym on weekends, but barely remembered any of the names of the people with whom he played racquetball. He also said that he found much of their conversation dull. There were so many exciting things going on in his life that listening to them talk about their petty concerns annoyed him. On the other hand, Brad wished he had some close friends in his life. The problem is that you can't have close friends without putting forth the effort necessary to make friends and maintain them.

I gave Brad the following homework: He was to spend two weeks showing interest in all the people he met. His job was to ask something about themselves, listen to their concerns, and pay attention to their stories. He might open up a conversation by asking where they were from, or complimenting their outfits and asking where they bought them, or asking their opinions.

Something profound happened for Brad during that two-week period. He expected that he would spend a lot of time waiting for people to finish talking. Instead, he felt connected to people, and less lonely and isolated than he had ever felt. By allowing people to fully express themselves, people became more interested in him and in his daily affairs, which invigorated him into sharing his thoughts.

Making your friends happy also means making time for them. In our active lives, time is one of our most precious commodities. How we spend our time is indicative of what is important to us. But, even when we do nothing, it seems laden with stress because we are constantly aware of what we "should" be doing. And when we take time out to relax or watch television, we often feel guilty. It is very hard to prioritize how we should spend our time because there is so much to accomplish and we are always behind!

But there is one area of your life that you must include in your weekly schedule, and that is spending time with friends. Your environmental stability needs good friendships to keep you on an even keel. You need friends to bounce ideas off of, to support your decisions, and to make you think clearer on important issues. No matter how limited your time, you need to select a day of the week and create a standing appointment with each friend. Whether you just meet for coffee, go out together, or even just talk on the telephone, you need to make time to keep the relationship healthy and strong.

You must also be supportive of your friends during rough times. Many people give only when it is convenient. We are perfectly content to send our friends birthday cards or lend them our travel alarm clocks. But when it comes to helping them clear out their desks after they've been fired, or driving them to the mechanic after an accident, or bringing food over to them when they're sick, many people feel that they are too busy to make the sacrifice.

And while many people don't want to be inconvenienced, still others are afraid of having advantage taken of them. *What if you keep giving, and they keep taking?* This is a valid concern, and if you are in this type of relationship, it may be a friendship that you might consider ending. On the other hand, you must have realized by now how important it is to work toward being the type of friend who is supportive during rough times. In turn you will be able to depend on your friends when you need them. Your objective is to be the best person you can be. Not only will this make you a better catch, but it will also create closer relationships with others.

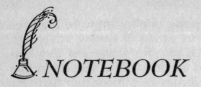

NOTEBOOK

- List your friends (do not include acquaintances).

- How does this list make you feel?

- Why do you choose the friends that you do? (What is the benefit to you?)

- In what ways can you be more friendly and giving?

- Do you make time for your friends?

Career

Most people admit to a certain amount of anxiety associated with the future of their jobs. No matter how good things are, there is always that nagging fear that they could get worse. Living with this constant anxiety makes us feel as if we are victims of the whims of our superiors. This stress can be unhealthy for our emotional stability. Our job is where we spend most of our waking hours, and having an environment that could disappear is certainly bound to make us feel unstable. That is why it is very important to focus on how *you* control your career.

In this chapter, you will learn the exact actions to take to be the best employee possible. By focusing on these tools, you will not only maximize your value to a company, you will also increase your own stability by having more control over your environment. And by doing everything to the best of your ability, you will lessen your anxiety and fear of the future. Even if you lose your job, you will know it was because of circumstances beyond your control.

Focus on Goals

First, focus on your goals. Where do you want to be in five years? For some people, such as doctors, lawyers, or other professionals, their career paths are pretty much set. But for the rest of us who may not have such clearly defined paths, deciding where we want to be in five years may be a bit more difficult.

Brenda finished college with a degree in psychology and began her career as the community relations director of a local charity organization. After two years, she was hired by one of the benefactors of the organization to run his real estate office. After four years, she worked her way up to be one of the top brokers at the firm. When real estate became difficult to sell, she decided to go into advertising sales for a national magazine, and has been doing it for three years. When I sat down with Brenda to make a five-year plan, she had no idea what she would want to be doing. She was successful in her current job, but she knew that she didn't want to be doing it for another five years.

Brenda and I brainstormed and came up with a few ideas. Brenda set her sights on either being the regional manager of her company, starting her own advertising sales company, or even starting her own real estate firm. After much discussion, Brenda confessed that her biggest dream is to have her own magazine. Though this idea seemed farfetched in the beginning, Brenda figured that if other people had done it, maybe she could, too. So she wrote down that her goal was to own her own magazine in five years.

It's amazing how once you write down your five-year goal, you are so much more aware of available opportunities. Within one month of writing down this goal, Brenda's boss asked her to write a small article on the changes in magazine advertising over the past decade. This gave Brenda lots of background information about what it would take to run her own magazine! Her goal also put Brenda's career in a new perspective. Instead of going through the day's work aimlessly, Brenda now had a mission that excited her! Go to your notebook and make your own five-year goal. Write down many different ideas, and then pick the idea that is most exciting to you, no matter how impractical it may seem.

Once you decide on a goal, make a plan as to how you can best accomplish it. You can start by researching the ways others have achieved goals similar to yours. Read biographies, speak with people who are where you want to be and learn from their mistakes and experiences.

Note what changes you may need to make in your current situation to progress toward your goal. For instance, Brenda may want to take a journalism course, or she may want to subscribe to a dozen magazines to examine the different styles of writing. She may want to spend some of her time in the editorial department of her office to see what really goes on behind the scenes. Or, she may want to share her idea with a business associate that might make a good partner in the project. But one thing is for sure, if Brenda doesn't go after what she wants, it certainly won't come after her!

It is also important to ask yourself *why* you want a particular goal. Do you want more money? More job security? A sense of accomplishment? The prestige involved? Knowing why you are doing something will give you the motivation to continue to chase your dream.

Determining a goal is not easy if you have no idea what you want to do in life. Some people take any job as a way to make money until they figure out what they really want from a career. Or they take a job that is a stepping stone to where they want to be. Or they take a job because they are qualified for it rather than wanting it. In all these cases, no one is able to commit to a job because the job is seen as a transition. This is a problem. If people spend most of their waking hours doing something halfheartedly, they can't help but feel a sense of futility in their lives. Their environment is unstable because they aren't totally committed to what they are doing.

Thus your next step to securing your job is to commit to it, regardless if it is a long-range goal or not. That means that you commit to do your best no matter how much you like or dislike your job. Rather than doing poor work because you really don't care about your work, you work to the best of your ability. The advantages of making such a commitment are many. One, you will have an invigorating workday because you will be stretching your capabilities to the maximum. Two, you will gain a sense of power over your own life and pride in your own abilities. And three, you will gain practice at performing optimally, which will help you to excel once you do have the job that maximizes your potential.

Opportunities seem to come to those who do the best with what they have. Why would someone hire a halfhearted employee away from their job? Maybe the chance of a lifetime will pass you by because someone considering you for a job noticed how little you dedicated yourself to your current employer. And maybe a possible spouse saw how uncommitted you were to your work and feared that you would show the same lack of enthusiasm in a relationship. Making this commitment to your current job will also help you see your five-year goal more clearly and open doors to opportunities because you will stand out from the crowd.

As an actress, Martha played the lead in several plays. She has wanted to be an actress since she was a young child, but so far, she hasn't had any big breaks. She dedicates much of her time to acting, but since it does not pay the bills, Martha also works as a secretary at an insurance agency. She does not like her job, nor does she have many friends at work. She spends most of her days watching the clock until it is time to leave and go off to acting class or rehearsal.

Since acting is Martha's primary focus, it is completely understandable that her secretarial job does not interest her. But Martha doesn't realize the enormous cost to herself of spending most of her time at a job to which she is apathetic. She is spending most of her days as a mediocre employee, doing as little as she can. This is not healthy for her self-esteem, nor is it healthy for her acting profession. This mediocrity will eventually spill over into her acting career. Instead Martha can make a commitment to her secretarial job and put forth the effort to be the best secretary possible. In the long run, Martha will not only feel better about herself, she will also be strengthening her potential for excellence—an asset which will prove valuable in every area of her life.

Be Dependable

Being dependable means getting things done. This is completely obvious, but an incredibly rare occurrence. People have a natural aversion to getting things done. The moment we are told to do something, we naturally don't want to do it. Given that our livelihood is dependent on how we get things done, this can present a little bit of a problem. Rick, one of the most successful businessmen I know, told me the secret to his success is not that he's more brilliant than his competitors, it is because projects and papers moved across his desk at twice the speed of his co-workers. Whether a simple memo about a new drinking fountain or a corporate takeover, he handles them with expedience that produces immediate results.

The lesson Rick taught me was invaluable. I actually began playing a game with myself to see how many items I could take from my "in" basket to my "out" basket in the course of a day. This game helped me return phone calls that I would have otherwise put off, R.S.V.P. to events on the same day that I received invitations, and allowed me the pleasure of leaving the office at the end of the day knowing that I had done as much work as possible. The human mind is expandable. The more you demand of yourself, the more you will be able to accomplish.

Being dependable also means following directions. People have a habit of listening to an instruction, interpreting it the way they want to, and producing a result different than what was asked for. Jan has been a secretary for eight years. She has never been promoted. Her bosses say she is too slow. Jan is upset about this since she tries her best to get work out on time and often works through lunch to finish her assignments. But she has resigned herself to the fact that her abilities are limited.

I had the opportunity to work with Jan on a volunteering project. A group of us were sitting around a big table, and Jan would take our ideas and input them into the computer. We were putting together an invitation for an event and I found it very frustrating to work with her. I would point to a line and tell her that it would look better centered. Jan would come back with the whole invitation centered. Someone would suggest we try putting the donors' names on the back, and she put them on the back flap of the envelope. Each time a direction was given, she would do what she thought we meant. Jan is as fast a typist as any other secretary in her office; what slows her down is the constant redoing of her work. The most important part of following directions is to understand them. Better to ask ten questions and do it right once, than to spend a lot of time doing it wrong.

Many people believe it is their job to input their own ideas rather than be paid just to take orders.

But if your ideas override the original directions, and you input them without authority, you will never be successful in your endeavors. Training oneself to follow directions is quite a challenge. I remember in grade school our teacher handed out a piece of paper with twenty tasks on it. The first task said to read the entire piece of paper before beginning any other tasks. The second task asked that we draw three triangles in the upper right hand corner of the page. For the third task we had to draw a circle on the back of the paper with three dots in it. It was quite a fun worksheet, and the whole class was busy at work following all of the directions very diligently. Except one person. Tammy Black sat at her desk reading a book. After twenty minutes, the teacher asked Tammy to read task number twenty aloud to the class. It read, "Do none of the aforementioned tasks." Only one person followed the simplest of instructions. Incidentally, it is amusing to know that the ability to follow directions may have something to do with the ability to succeed: Tammy went to Harvard University and then became a highly skilled physician.

Question what keeps you from following directions. We all have a little rebellion in us that makes us not want to do what someone demands of us. Being dependable and following directions means getting to work on time. It means not taking sick days when you're not sick. It means asking questions to make sure that you do things right. It means doing things that maybe you don't feel like doing. It means voicing your opinions about how things should be done before doing something differently than the way it was requested. Analyze what stops you from following directions and then commit yourself to doing things differently in the future. You will be contributing greatly to your environmental stability.

One more way to increase your dependability is to make concrete plans on how you want to accomplish something, and then stick to those plans. Often, people get so caught up with their day-to-day work that they can't see the big picture. That is why it is important to take time out of your busy schedule on a regular basis to make those plans. For instance, rather than becoming frantic every time there is no more copier paper, make a concrete plan to reorder office supplies every two weeks. Make a checklist of all supplies that you might need, and then write on your calendar, "supply day," so that you will remember to order supplies on that day. By creating a concrete plan, projects seem much less overwhelming and you will find that you are much more dependable because you are able to accomplish more.

Maureen was overwhelmed with work. She owned a small clothing boutique that catered to an affluent clientele. When she finally met the man that she wanted to marry, she realized he was hesitant to propose marriage because he saw that she was spending too much time taking care of her very busy business. When a custom-made suit, skirt, or blouse was ordered, Maureen prided herself on her policy to deliver within two weeks. There was always a backlog of orders, and orders poured in all day long. This made her shop a very stressful place to work. The tailors were forever working overtime, which cost Maureen extra. The salesclerks felt that selling a suit was a mixed blessing—they would earn a commission, but they knew that every suit they sold would create more stress for Maureen. This was an unhealthy situation and, as a result, Maureen had a very high employee turnover.

Given how busy the shop was, Maureen never even had time to sit down to eat lunch, let alone find the time to create a concrete plan on how to make her shop more efficient. But she realized that she needed a better system if her future were to include a spouse, a family, and a career. Finally, a business consultant talked Maureen into taking four days off, after the holiday shopping season, to create a business plan. It was decided that all orders taken during the week would be written up and put in a box. On Mondays, the box would be turned over to the tailors who then had two weeks to produce the clothing. Maureen had to change her policy to a three-week delivery or less, but the pleasant atmosphere in her shop was well worth it. The tailors were able to schedule their work much more efficiently, shopping for materials every Tuesday instead of running around all week long, making Wednesday their cutting day, and so forth. The change was so dramatic that Maureen began taking time for lunch, she works only fifty hours per week instead of seventy, and has a lot more free time for her boyfriend! This concrete plan not only made Maureen's shop more efficient, it cut down the employee turnover, and also made everyone's life more enjoyable and satisfying. And to top it off, Maureen's boyfriend proposed!

Manage Relationships Well

The key to managing relationships is to be nice to everyone. This is so easy to accomplish yet it is one of the most overlooked success techniques. A wise woman once told me, "You pass the same people on the way down that you trampled over on the way up." Your success depends on every person you encounter. I heard a story from my friend who works at a large stock-brokerage house. The vice president of the firm was being considered for the position of chief executive officer. This man had never acknowledged the existence of the lobby receptionist, even though he passed her desk several times a day for two years. The receptionist, however, happened to be the sister of one of the board members. She made several remarks against the vice president, which ultimately influenced her brother and he in turn influenced the other board members to vote against him.

The man didn't get the job. You never know how someone can hurt or help you, so it is best to be nice to everyone.

Each work place has a pecking order. The foreman feels more important than the workers, the doctor feels more important than the nurses, the twenty-year employee feels more important than the new-comer. But in truth they all need each other to succeed. No matter what position you have, if you are friendly to everyone, you will have the best possible chance to succeed. Greet everyone in a friendly way. Go out of your way to help people. Don't be too proud to make the coffee once in a while. People appreciate small kindnesses. If someone gets stuck working late, offer to pick up dinner for them. Or sit and listen to the receptionist's troubles; it doesn't cost you anything, and she may help you out of a jam someday.

Try to remember what people said they were going to do over their weekend and ask them about it Monday morning. People like to be remembered. If someone asks you for a favor, don't do it grudgingly. Making someone feel obligated is worse than just saying no. Don't be afraid to go out of your way for someone, even if they don't return the favor. Also, don't forget to be friendly to your boss. There is a fine line between a business relationship and inappropriate personal closeness between employee and employer, but friendliness, kind words, and kind deeds are perfectly appropriate.

Learn to manage your business relationships by meeting your boss's needs. The lack of communication in relationships is astounding, but even more so in the very demanding relationship between a boss and his/her employee. The employee often feels that he/she can never please the boss, and the boss is forever balancing between making demands, giving praise, and giving criticism. This makes for a very awkward relationship, and it takes great skill to make it a harmonious one. We are all employees. Even if you don't have superiors because you are self-employed, then your customer is your boss. We all have to answer to someone, and the more we understand what needs there are, and how we can best meet them, the better we will satisfy and stabilize our working environment.

Denice is the office manager at a large law firm. She is very capable, but she has a dreadful relationship with her boss. He is a senior partner and doesn't have any time to meet with Denice on a regular basis. Therefore, there are continuous communication problems, and Denice is always blamed for her inability to produce the results her boss wants. Denice sees this primarily as her boss's fault for not taking the time to meet with her, for not making his needs more clear, and especially for having tantrums when everything doesn't turn out as he wants.

The first rule of being a successful employee is to recognize that it is not your boss's job to make you happy. Whether it is her boss's fault or not, if the relationship isn't working, Denice only has control over herself. To spend energy being angry and complaining to everyone is a fruitless exercise, and will surely come back to haunt her later. As the employee, it is Denice's job to make the situation workable. This may not be the fair way to allocate responsibility, but waiting for the boss to make this situation amenable will only make a bad problem worse. Since Denice's power lies in her own abilities, she decided to do some serious thinking until she could figure out how to best resolve this situation.

Denice sat down with her sister, who has a master's degree in business administration. The two of them talked about possible solutions for hours. They finally came up with a brilliant plan. On Friday mornings, Denice would place a weekly plan for the following week on her boss's desk. To the left of each item on the "To Do" list, she put an empty box for her boss to initial his approval. At the bottom of the list were several blank lines for him to jot in other items that Denice might have forgotten. Her boss would then leave this plan on Denice's desk for her by Monday morning. As you can probably imagine, this simple communication tool increased the office effectiveness by an enormous margin and heightened office morale. Her boss was quite pleased with this new plan, and in fact, it became a basis for weekly discussions. At one point Denice told him she realized he raised his voice when things weren't getting done efficiently, but when he yelled at her in front of the other employees it made it difficult for her to maintain any authority. Her boss apologized and agreed not to yell at her in front of others. These fabulous results were produced by Denice, who took responsibility for meeting her boss's needs rather than placing the blame elsewhere. By thinking things through thoroughly she figured out a solution to the situation and resolved it.

Handle problems with poise. Many people think that life is "supposed" to go perfectly. When a problem arises they get very upset. I once heard an artist say, "It's not how well you paint, but how well you correct your mistakes." In a business setting, how well you handle the problems that arise will make an enormous impact on the success of your work relationships. We all know people who lose their temper at the smallest hassle. These people are difficult to be around socially, much less in the workplace.

Handling problems with poise means that when the copier machine breaks down, you don't yell at the copier repairman. If your secretary forgot to mail a letter that was supposed to go out last week, don't make her feel like she is completely incompetent. Yelling at her will only make her feel worse and she is likely to make another big mistake. On the other hand, if you tell her that it's a mistake that anyone might have made, she will be grateful for your generosity, and work harder for you.

Next time a problem arises, think about how you can best handle it so that it works to your advantage. If you lose a major account, have a meeting to analyze what went wrong and plan to correct the problems rather than yelling at everyone involved. If your business partner is always late to work, rather than brooding about it, make an agreement that he/she come in late and stay late. If an employee quits, call a staff meeting to discuss it so that everyone feels like part of the team. Working toward being the kind of person who handles problems with poise will not only make you a more valuable employee, but it will also prepare you to be a good spouse. We are not practicing life, we are living it. You have only one chance to be the best you that you can be, and mastering the art of handling problems with poise will serve you in all areas of your life.

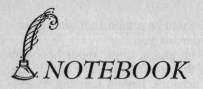

NOTEBOOK

- What do you want to be doing in five years?
- How do you plan to achieve this goal?
- Why do you want this goal?
- Do you have a plan for your future?
- How are your relationships with your co-workers?

Community

Most people see community involvement as an ancillary part of life. Once we have our careers going, our cars in working order, our houses cleaned, and our workout schedules perfected, then we will get involved in our communities. In order of priority it comes right behind sewing buttons on our shirt and rewriting addresses into a new book. But you should be aware that it is impossible to have a healthy, stable environment without being civically active. Being active moves you away from the natural tendency to be self-absorbed. Involving yourself with the welfare of others is one of the keys to happiness. It will also help you grow into the kind of person that you want to be: kind, considerate, and a contributing member of society.

Get Around

Start by going to as many community events as possible. Attend charity functions, political rallies, environmental lectures, or whatever else interests you. A baseball game does not count as a community event. A community event is one that is designed to improve the welfare of the community. Look in your local paper for organizations and ask your friends about events that they may attend. If you feel uncomfortable going alone, go with a friend, or better yet, call the organization and ask if they need volunteers. It's much easier to meet people when you are sitting behind a table giving out name tags than it is hovering in a corner! Many people are intimidated by large groups, but if you keep in mind that you just want to get to know a couple of people, your task becomes manageable. If you are trying to develop new friendships as part of your goal of creating a stable environment, community involvement is a great way to meet people with similar interests and concerns.

Wherever you go, get people's business cards, and write on the back of the card the date and the event you met them at, as well as any pertinent information about that person. Your objective should be to build a resource of people that becomes your own private "community." I guarantee that you will find yourself often flipping through your box of cards. Knowing a lot of people from many different fields not only gives you a network to support you in whatever you are doing, but it also makes you feel like you belong to your community.

My friend Pam, who has a business card box, was working on a big charity event. Two days before invitations to a fund-raiser were to be printed, the board decided they wanted to advertise door prizes on the invitation. Within four hours of phone work with her box on hand, Pam had secured twelve door prizes including a weekend for two at a fancy hotel!

Your network of sources presents a valuable way to put people together. People will call you to see if you know a good attorney, or if you have a plumber you trust, or to find out if you know anyone who organizes offices, or a banker. And when you refer business to people, they tend to refer business to you. This means they will refer customers to your business, or refer people to you for many reasons that will benefit you personally, and even more valuable, they may refer a possible spouse!

Join an Organization

There are three basic types of organizations you can join: a charitable volunteer group, a political activist group, or a religious organization. You can go to a few meetings to see which of these groups suits your needs and tastes. You can find out about meetings from friends or co-workers, or from advertisements in the calendar section of your local newspaper. Often there are special membership drives, which are great because they give a lot of information that will help you decide if you would like to join.

Charitable volunteer groups are easy to become involved in because they are so appreciative of all the help they can get! The best way to choose a charity is to join a group that you feel is a worthy cause, whether it is helping the homeless, saving the environment, educating children, or supporting the arts. If it is a cause that you feel strongly about, you are going to be more motivated to attend the meetings. You will also meet people who have similar interests. Being involved in the community means meeting the community, one person at a time.

Francine is the manager for a large retail store. She works very hard, and rarely arrives home before eight o'clock. When she attended my Get Married Now™ seminar, she said that she had only had one boyfriend for two months during the whole three years that she had been the manager. She was very determined to get married and realized that she had to change something about her lifestyle. I spoke extensively to Francine, and we discovered that she had two problems to solve. First, she needed to organize her schedule to be more conducive to meeting a husband. And second, she needed to become active in her community in order to work on being the kind of person that a mate would find attractive.

Francine could not see a way to work less hours, but after doing some research about community organizations, she found a singles group that met for a business lunch every other week. The group raised money for cancer research and Francine felt that if she met a man who was volunteering his time, he would probably be a caring person. She also wanted to develop her own ability to care. She found that as a manager, she had an "all business" attitude with her employees that carried over into the rest of her relationships. She also wanted to develop a more friendly attitude and to hone her communication skills. Francine has not only made a great step in terms of her future by putting herself in a place where she will meet a husband, but at the same time she has made a huge step toward creating a more stable environment by being active in her community. This will certainly make her a much greater catch!

Political activist groups may take you some time to choose. It is important that you not only believe in their politics, but you must also support their methods of achieving their objectives. You must also be willing to stand up to the opposition. It takes a bit of research to find the right organization. You can ask friends, do library research, or look in the local paper, but try to attend several meetings before you make a commitment to the group. Political groups might be national organizations uniting for a common cause, organizations supporting a particular candidate, or local organizations interested in local issues. During election time, political organizations are great fun, but year-round, they try to make a difference in their communities. Belonging to this type of group is a valuable way to support your community.

Religious organizations can be a great way to create an instant social circle. These organizations bring together people of similar backgrounds, and many of their activities involve planning and attending lots of fun events such as dances and trips. There are always special events for all of the religious holidays, fundraisers, and special meals. These organizations are also a great source for finding new friends or a mate. Call the churches or synagogues in your area to get information or a newsletter. Then attend a few services, events, or classes to see how you like the organization. If you can't find a group that interests you, consider starting your own! Call the clergyman and tell him your idea and ask for a few people's names to help you get the group started. Community involvement means putting out effort for your community.

Have Staying Power

Show up at the weekly meeting of whatever organization you join. So many people get overly enthusiastic when they first join an organization only to disappear within a few weeks. Giving to the community means giving even when you don't feel like it. Every organization is made up of eighty percent of the people who enjoy the benefits of the organization, and twenty percent of the people who do all of the work. It would be nice if this could be changed, but again, all we have control over is ourselves. Being a good catch and a responsible person means being part of that twenty percent. Just by showing up to the regular meetings, you lend your support to the organization and become one of the insiders.

Be an anchor in your organization. If events are poorly planned and the turnouts are always dismal, run for president. Be a cheerleader when morale is low. During difficult times, a person of vision, one who remembers the purpose of the organization, can completely transform a bad situation. You can call up all of the important players and rally their support back to the cause. Or you could partner up with a difficult person no one wants to work with to resurrect a failing event. Being an anchor means maintaining your commitment during rough times.

Finally, recruit new members. The challenge of bringing in new members is often left to one person. This person, working twenty-four hours a day, could not possibly network with as many people as a whole organization dedicated to recruitment. If all of the members commit to bringing in one member a year, or one a month, the job then becomes fairly easy. If you make a commitment to recruit new members, it will keep your organization vital and growing. It will also sharpen your people skills. Because you will be forced to "sell" the organization to possible members you will need to be at your friendliest and most cordial. Your shyness will be alleviated, you will have a topic on hand to discuss, thereby avoiding awkward silences, and with time you will see how much easier it is to talk to strangers.

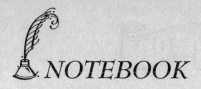

NOTEBOOK

- What stops you from going to events, getting people's numbers, or introducing people to each other?

- List possible charitable, politically active, or religious groups you would like to join.

- Are you now willing to attend community functions or become more involved with their daily activities?

Hobbies

Hobbies often help stabilize our environment. Life is full of difficulties and a hobby is a great way to relax. Hobbies are also a great way to meet people and to help you maintain a balanced, well-rounded life. A hobby also makes you more interesting to others. You have more to talk about, and you are more enthusiastic about your life.

Choosing a hobby may be easy for you if you have had one in the past. If you once learned French in your spare time, then getting back into it will be easy. If you used to play tennis, picking up the racquet won't be so difficult. If you already have a collection of baseball cards, adding to your collection will be fun. But for people who never had a hobby, you should know that you can choose one where you are continuously learning about something, a hobby where you collect something, or one that involves physical activity. Your choice will depend on what you enjoy.

Learn Something

If you ever wondered why there are different stars in the summer than there are in the winter, then how about taking a course in astronomy? If you always wanted to write the great American novel, why not enroll in a writing class? If you have ever wanted to learn how to bake sourdough bread, how about sitting beside a chef and watching? Unfortunately, our curiosity is often suppressed by our busy adult lives. But if you pass up an opportunity to enhance your life or deny yourself a learning experience then you will be making yourself a willing slave to your work and your "To Do" list. We feel as if we never really have time to ourselves to do whatever we feel like. And because our lives are packed with things we "should" do, if we do take time for ourselves, we often feel guilty about it. But taking the time for a hobby is perfectly justified because you are taking the time out to balance your life, and maybe meet someone who shares your passions for a specific interest. Two very worthwhile endeavors!

There are many types of hobbies. You can learn how to knit, sew, repair a car, arrange flowers, make pastries or stained glass windows, paint, sing, write calligraphy, play bridge, or grow tomatoes. The possibilities are endless! If this sounds like childhood revisited, good! The one thing all hobbies have in common is that they make you forget about time, worries, and all your pressures! And these restorative powers cannot be underestimated!

The best way to choose a hobby, if you don't have one in mind, is to go to the library. There is such an ample selection of books on hobbies that no doubt you will find something that strikes your fancy. Once you have an idea of what you want to pursue, you can see if there are classes taught at area schools, or organizations that cater to that hobby.

There are also a variety of subjects you can enroll in at your local college or community center. You can learn about a particular historical period, a particular animal, product manufacturing, gemstones, new medical technology, the environment, trivia, or science fiction. You can even learn more about your religion by studying its history and philosophy, or learn more about fulfilling your potential.

You can learn about other fields such as poetry, psychology, legal issues, gardening, deep sea diving, the air force, children's education, designing traffic patterns, scriptwriting, plant life, or farm animals. Classes are the best way to learn about these areas.

Jim was interested in photography. He started by taking a class on the history of photography. He learned about the chemical process and about great photographers and how they progressed in their careers. Jim was so fascinated that he began collecting photography books, and eventually tried his hand at this craft. His apartment is now filled with his own photographs and works by other photographers. He spends many weekends traveling to photograph interesting landscapes, and he even sold a photo that was later used as a postcard!

Collect Something

Collecting is also great fun. Once you get started, it's hard to stop! You will get addicted to the item that you collect! Family and friends also get into the fun of it by picking up a particular collectible item for birthdays, holidays, and any special occasions. And your collection doesn't need to cost very much as the following ideas will make clear.

Some people collect old things. This includes antique furniture, toy trains from the turn of the century, original poetry manuscripts, books, cereal cartons, cashmere gloves, spoons, letters from famous persons, clocks, bottles, leather goods, Indian artifacts, fossils, buttons, candlesticks, dolls, fans, perfume bottles, or baseball helmets. These items might be found in antique or secondhand shops. Or, you might find antique dealers who advertise in newspapers or in the phone book. There are organizations that cater to collectors, and this is a great way to meet people! Research these organizations to find out if there are shows in your area for the item that you collect. Once you get started, you will see that there is a whole world out there in which you can take part. It is a very rewarding hobby, and it will be a pleasure to share your collection with visitors.

Other people collect items of our popular culture: comic books, special beer bottles, matches, stamps, foreign coins, anything with an elephant on it, glass soda bottles, maps of every state, political buttons, Southwestern art, little troll dolls, watches, airline swizzle sticks, music, pens, books on alligators, rubber stamps, refrigerator magnets, or anything in miniature. There are so many popular things to collect that you might have a hard time choosing one item.

You can collect anything that suits your fancy! This might include butterfly wings, bird feathers, theater ticket stubs, charity ball dinner menus, signatures of basketball players, magazine articles on changing cultural norms, embroidered doilies, teacups and saucers, dried gourds, funny greeting cards, computer software programs, original cartoon drawings, sepia-toned photographs, or chess sets. Learning about your item is a great way to further your enjoyment, and it makes it more interesting when you show your collection to others. Also, remember that everyone may not share your obsession so try not to bore every person that walks into your house! But most everyone will enjoy learning about something that you are enthusiastic about.

Do Something

Sports activities make great hobbies. This might include softball, tennis, swimming, skiing, racquetball, aerobics, horseback riding, running, surfing, bowling, bike riding, sailing, volleyball, race driving, canoeing, or hiking. Choosing a sport may be based on what you have liked in the past, or maybe you want to try something completely different. A good way to get started is to take lessons in order to learn the basics. Finding a friend to participate with you can also be a good way to get started. The key is to get out the first time, and to set aside time in your schedule every week to keep up your hobby. The purpose of your sports hobby is purely to have fun.

Brent was a great tennis player when he was in high school. He was on the varsity team, and even went to the state championships. But after high school, he stopped playing, and now he is afraid to pick up a racquet for fear that his skills would be laughable. So year after year goes by, and he doesn't take advantage of a hobby that he enjoys. But if Brent were able to see that it didn't make any difference what his skill level was, his life would be much enriched by a weekly game of tennis. Not only would he meet many more people, but he would have an area outside of work he was passionate about, something that made him happier, and a better catch.

You can also have a hobby of observing events. You can observe exhibits at art museums and antique shows. You can make a monthly habit of going to the theater, the ballet, concerts, car shows, dance recitals, history museums, zoos, or country fairs. These types of hobbies are great because you can always bring a friend along. Go to many different types of events to start off with, and when you find an area of interest that appeals to you, do some research on the topic. It is so much more enjoyable to go to an exhibit of ancient artifacts if you have read a historical novel on the time period, or a review of the exhibit in the newspaper, or studied diagrams of burial sites in a textbook.

There are still other hobbies to become involved in which are very social in nature. These include playing bridge, square dancing, playing bingo, singing in a choral group, archery, acting in plays, playing an instrument, coaching a little league team, being a docent at a museum, or bird watching. These hobbies are great because you get to know the participants well, and you can develop lasting friendships. Given that so much of our identity in society is determined by what we do for a living, having this other outlet where no one really cares what you do is a refreshing break, and allows you to show another side of yourself. And this is great for your self-expression.

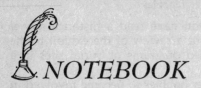

NOTEBOOK

- Make a list of hobbies you might enjoy.
- What will be your first step in starting a new hobby?
- Now go out and enjoy it!

Part Three

CHARACTER TRAITS

If you have followed many of the suggestions in this book, you have come a long way so far! You have learned how to overcome past patterns, how to stabilize your emotions, and how to create a stable environment for yourself. If you do nothing else, you have already made yourself into a better catch! Now we are going to work on character traits that will make you an *irresistible* catch! There is nothing more powerful and alluring than a sterling character!

I am often asked by my students how to be a better person, both for finding a mate, and for their own personal growth. The answer is right in this chapter: by working on your character traits! There are hundreds of character traits, but I am going to discuss the five that will be the most valuable for you to be a great catch. They are kindness, compassion, honesty, speaking carefully, and humility.

Some of what you learn in this section may take years to integrate into your life. But remember, you are working on fulfilling your potential. No one has mastered every one of these character traits in their entirety. The challenge is to become as strong in each trait as possible, and to continue developing your traits for the rest of your life. Not only will this make you a better catch and a better spouse, but it will also make your life more meaningful and fulfilled as you grow and fulfill your potential.

Kindness

At a charity dinner, I had the occasion to sit next to a famous celebrity. We chatted mostly about insignificant matters, but when a waiter was rude to one of the guests, everyone at our table began to discuss it. The celebrity said that she tried to be kind to everyone, which was especially challenging when she was swamped with fans. But she said that she was surprised at the lack of kindness that she encountered daily.

She recounted a story about a time when she was on the telephone with a rude receptionist who kept putting her on hold. She asked to speak with a certain gentleman, and without saying, "Could you please hold," the receptionist just pressed the hold button. When the receptionist came back she said, "He's on the other line, you'll have to wait," and again pressed the hold button without letting the caller say a word. As this celebrity merely wanted to leave a quick message, she hung up and dialed the number again. When the receptionist recognized her voice, she hollered into the phone, "Now you will go to the end of the line behind all of the other callers," and again put her on hold without letting her say a word! The celebrity was so incensed that she hung up, called back, and instead of asking for the gentleman, she said, "This is [she announced her name, which the receptionist recognized] and I have been holding for Mr. Smith." The receptionist, realizing that this was the voice of the woman she had put on hold so rudely, went into a tirade of apologies, told the celebrity what a big fan she was, and even had the nerve to ask the celebrity to send her a signed photograph!

The celebrity said that what bothered her most about this incident was that the woman changed her manner the moment she discovered a celebrity was on the line. As if she deserved to be treated more humanely than others. She said that similar incidents happen to her all the time. People start out rudely or thoughtlessly, and the moment they find out who she is, they treat her like a queen. Disgusted, she said every person should be treated kindly and with respect. We are all living, breathing people with feelings and rights.

You should be kind to everyone, from the janitor to the chairman of the board, with equal enthusiasm. It means being kind when you don't feel like it and when it might be inconvenient. Kindness means imagining yourself in the other person's place, and treating him or her as you would hope to be treated. If someone comes to you for help, it is easy to come up with fifty excuses as to why you can't help. You don't have the money to lend, you can't be late for work, you don't have the time, etc. But if you put yourself in another's shoes, or think of the fact that maybe this is your personal test to see how kind you can be, then maybe kindness will prevail. If you think of kindness as a muscle, the kinder you are, the stronger your ability to be kind becomes. It is important to be kind to everyone, from a stranger, to a friend, to a family member. And when a potential mate happens to catch you in an act of kindness, he or she is much more likely to be interested in you. The more of a habit kindness becomes for you, the more likely someone will catch you behaving at your very best.

Acts of kindness include every way that a person might extend himself for another. That might mean visiting the sick, comforting mourners, bringing joy to a bridal pair, bringing peace between others, returning lost property, or even being nice to a phone salesman. (Yes, you read this correctly—it is *never* okay to hang up the phone on someone, even if they are rude, and even if they deserve it.) Some people may really test your ability to be kind, but that is how you strengthen your muscle.

Acts of kindness also include acts of charity: giving money to the poor, treating a homeless person with dignity, buying goods from the poor even if you don't really need them, or donating your time to a charitable organization. And kindness is most worthy when it is carried out with love, not grudgingly.

Hospitality is also a very important aspect of kindness. Hosting people in your home takes great kindness. And the kinder you are to your guests, the more valuable the experience. Help your guests off with their coats, get them refreshments right away, fill their glasses when they become almost empty, and if they spill coffee on your rug, act like you aren't upset; this will alleviate their feelings of guilt or embarrassment. If you think of all of your acts of kindness as building on one another, like savings in a bank, you can see that being kind can become addictive! The more kind acts you perform, the stronger this character trait becomes.

Many people feel that if they perform a kind act, such as visit a sick person in the hospital, then they have "paid their dues" for the month. Others feel that as long as they don't do harm, they are off the hook. One should strive every day to do something righteous and kind. Being kind isn't just a nice trait that would be better to have than to not have. The trait of being kind is an absolute necessity to living a fulfilled, satisfied life. One should feel regret if a single day passes without performing an act of kindness. It is one of the character traits most responsible for long-term happiness.

Many of my students report having low self-esteem. There is no better cure for this than performing an act of kindness. It is impossible to feel bad about yourself after you have visited a sick person in the hospital, helped a stranger put their fallen groceries back into their bag, or returned five dollars to the store clerk who accidentally gave you too much change. If you are ever feeling bad about yourself, try doing something nice for someone. Pick up the phone and call your great-aunt in the nursing home. Clean out the old newspapers from your apartment lobby. Or write a letter to a sick friend. You can be sure that you will not only cheer yourself up, but your self-esteem will be raised a few notches. Do this often enough, and you won't ever report having low self-esteem again!

And don't make light of any act of kindness, no matter how small. Everything, in its own way, has merit and value, and sometimes we cannot judge how our kindness will affect others. Once I was in the grocery store and I happened to comment to the woman behind me that she was wearing a beautiful sweater. A few minutes later, she tapped me on the shoulder and said, "You know it's been a very hard time for me recently. I want you to know that you really lifted my spirits."

With kindness, you have the power to raise another person's spirits, to bring joy and comfort, to calm nerves, and to make someone feel good. In fact, many acts of kindness are so easy that you can perform them without any effort. And the truth is that you have so much to gain in terms of raising your self-esteem, and improving your character traits, not to mention how valuable kindness is in terms of attracting a mate.

Practice Being Kind

Make a "kindness" list. This might include being nice to the receptionist at your office, calling your grandmother, giving money to charity, cooking a meal for your roommate, writing an overdue letter to a relative, apologizing to a friend for a wrongdoing, visiting a nursing home to cheer up the residents, giving a surprise gift to a friend, giving your secretary the afternoon off, forgiving someone for something they don't deserve forgiveness for, helping your sister clean out her messy closets, or smiling at every stranger you pass.

The longer your list, the better. And don't worry if the list makes you feel overburdened; just remember that the process of merely making this list is a powerful exercise toward becoming kinder. Your thinking patterns will start to change and you will see all the opportunities around you to spread good cheer. This should give you a sense of well-being and happiness.

Choose some of the kind acts that you will do in the coming week. You might want to choose just one or two items. Write these acts down, and plan on which days this week you will perform these acts. Then, write down how you felt after each act. Did you feel good about yourself? Was it easier or more difficult than you thought? Did you feel afterward it was a big waste of time? Did you feel angry that the person wasn't grateful for how much effort you expended for them? Write down your feelings. With more acts of kindness, and more experience flexing this muscle, your feelings about these acts will change, and their value to you will change also.

If someone is especially undeserving of your kindness, writing about it will diffuse some of the anger you might feel. For example, Marsha, knowing her co-worker was going to be late for a basketball game, said that she would stay late to finish the paperwork. That evening the boss also stayed late, which made Marsha look very good. Marsha truly had made a kind gesture toward her co-worker, but the next day he accused her of taking advantage of the situation to look like the better employee. Marsha was very angry and upset. She had tried to be kind, and he completely misinterpreted her intentions. This may happen to you. If it does, writing down your feelings will be a cathartic release. But under no circumstances should you let this type of incident sway you from your determination to be as kind a person as you can be.

Make Kindness Easier

Make a list of times when it is hardest for you to be kind. Maybe when you are in a big rush, you don't hold the elevator door for someone running down the hall. Maybe when you are preoccupied with work, you forget to greet people as you pass them in the office. Maybe when someone is rude, you can't bring yourself to be kind to them. We all have our challenges, but the better you understand your moments of weakness, the better you can plan on how to be kind in the face of a difficult situation.

It's also fun to invent games that help you to be kind and to diffuse anger you may feel throughout the day. I used to get extremely upset and angry if someone cut me off when I was driving. I never went so far as to seek revenge, but I sure felt like it! Obviously I could not avoid others cutting me off if I wished to continue driving, so I invented a game to help me be kind. I pretended that the driver who cut me off was really a secret guardian who was there to protect me. You see, I was actually supposed to be in a horrible accident at the next intersection, and this wonderful person, by cutting me off, slowed me down just enough to avoid the accident. Ridiculous, yes. Does it work, absolutely. Now, when someone cuts me off, I do not get upset for even one second! This may sound like nothing to you, but it is a big accomplishment for me, not to mention how much more pleasant it is for passengers in my car. And by the way, you should know that this change took me over six months to accomplish. Each time I was cut off, I was more and more able to deal with it in a kind manner.

I have also invented a game I call the "thirty-second game," which helps me find the time to be kind when I am in a rush. The idea is that every time you are in a rush, and there is a situation which requires your kindness, you are gifted thirty seconds. For example, let's say you are on your way to see your boss. It's 1:58 P.M. and you are supposed to be there by 2:00 P.M. On your way to his office you find a co-worker cleaning his dropped files off of the floor. Now, if you help out your co-worker, somehow you will regain the thirty seconds. Either the elevator will show up right away when it typically takes one minute, your boss will show up to the meeting late, or you will be late, and when you explain why, you will win points with your boss. Inventing a game like this *before* you are faced with a difficult situation will give you a great deal of power in overcoming your challenges to being kind.

Colleen always had a difficult time being kind when she was under a deadline at work. She became very short-tempered with people, and mostly went into her office and shut the door during deadline. She decided that she wanted to be kinder during her stressful times, so she invented this game for herself. Every time she talked kindly to someone during a deadline, she would put a little *x* on her calendar. When she accumulated twenty of them, she rewarded herself with a piece of costume jewelry from the vendor on the sidewalk!

This little game not only worked to curb her short-temperedness, but it had an advantage she could not have foreseen. One day when she was on a very tight deadline and under a lot of pressure, she noticed that she had eighteen x's on her calendar. She decided that she was going to earn a piece of jewelry by the end of the day no matter how pressured she felt! It just so happened that the computer salesman she decided to say something kind to happened to be single, and interested in her. Those first words of kindness she spoke to him started a relationship that may just lead to marriage!

Another game that you might play if you have a difficult time being kind to people who are rude is "The ruder you are, the nicer I'll be, and boy will you be sorry" game. This game has obvious advantages and can be quite enjoyable. After years of playing it however, the game turns into "The ruder you are, the nicer I'll be, and maybe you'll be inspired to be nice" game. Both of these games will help you behave kindly when you really don't feel like it! Inventing your own game for your own situation is challenging. You'll know you've hit upon the right game with the right rules if it makes you crack a smile when you think of it.

Acknowledge yourself for every act of kindness. It is not always easy to be kind. Others around you are not always kind, your patience is not always accessible, people misinterpret your kindness, or there are times when you neglect to help a little old lady across the street because you are rushed. Don't berate yourself. Just try to do the best you can always, and you will have no regrets.

Sometimes we are going through difficult emotional times, and the last thing we have energy to do is to reach out to someone else. If you can't go visit a sick relative, acknowledge yourself for even making the effort to call her. If you really do not have time to help your friend move to a new apartment over the weekend, acknowledge yourself for offering to help her unpack during the week. If you aren't able to go to a friend's birthday party, acknowledge yourself for having the thoughtfulness to mail her a gift ahead of time.

Even if you have been working hard on being kind, and then end up being very unkind to someone, don't feel like you are a horrible person. Try to rectify that situation if you can, but remember, you are working on a noble mission. Being kind is very challenging, and takes a great deal of thought and effort. It gets easier over time, and the rewards are plentiful, but you must remember that you are in this challenging pursuit for the long haul. You are pursuing a lifetime of kindness, not so that on one particular day you can feel good about yourself, but so that you can become the kind of person who is happy, fulfilled, and leads a meaningful life.

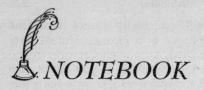

NOTEBOOK

- Make a "kindness list" of all the kind acts you can think of.

- Choose some of these acts of kindness to do in the coming week.

- After you have performed these acts, write down how you felt.

- What kind act could you do every day?

Compassion

One Saturday morning in June, a dozen people sat on the benches of a quiet little park. Streams of sunlight poured through the trees, and in the cloudless sky, flocks of birds enjoyed the gentle breeze. An elderly woman sat holding her bag on her lap, looking at the flowers with a smile, two young men sat reading their newspapers, and a man with a cane dozed with his head resting on his chest. As a dog chased a squirrel up a tree it barked wildly, but the people didn't seem to notice. Into the park came a couple in their mid-thirties with a young boy. They plopped onto a bench closest to the gate, and the boy sat at their feet.

As a breeze blew through the park, the people who had been sitting in silence for over an hour inspected the family. The man had a forlorn look on his face. He was staring at a spot on the ground, and didn't seem to know where he was. The woman was resting her head on his shoulder. When a little girl rode by on her bicycle, the boy jumped up with a scream and started running after her. He shouted profanities and flapped his arms vigorously. The elderly woman shot the family an angry look, but they weren't paying attention. She shook her head in disgust and looked away.

As the boy yanked flowers out of the ground, he began singing some sort of chant. One of the two men wrinkled his newspaper noisily, hoping to get the father's attention, but the father just stared blankly into space. Soon the people in the park were united in their fury at the family. They shared nods of disapproval and whispered angry comments, hoping the couple would hear.

Finally, a brave middle-aged woman stood up and went over to them. "Don't you think you should do something about your child?" she said with a note of irritation in her voice. The man, as if shaken from a dream, looked up at the woman. "What do you mean?" he asked. "Your son is acting like a wild animal," she replied. The young woman looked to the far end of the park, saw the boy standing on a bench throwing pebbles at people passing by, and hid her face in her husband's shoulder. "I'm sorry, ma'am," the man said. "You're right. I guess we're not handling our situation too well. You see, we're the boy's foster parents and the agency informed all of us today that they're going to take little Timmy away and place him in a permanent home."

Give People the Benefit of the Doubt

You have the power to judge others in any way you want. Our natural inclination is to judge people on our first impression, which is often very inaccurate. That is why in giving people the benefit of the doubt, you might first consider possible explanations for others' behavior. This can be challenging. It is hard to imagine ourselves sitting in that park and not getting as angry as everyone else. The challenge is to be able to think instead, "Boy they are being very inconsiderate, but maybe there is some circumstance that I don't know about that makes them act that way." And if a fellow parkgoer leans over and says, "Can you believe how ill-behaved that child is? And the father just sits there doing nothing!" you might be able to say, "I think you are right, but you never know, they might have a difficult family life or maybe he's an uncle so he doesn't want to scold him." Inventing explanations is the first step toward being compassionate to people who, at first impression, don't deserve it.

There is an old story about a man who worked for a wealthy farmer for three years. At the end of that time, he went to the farmer and asked for his wages. "Our contract is up, and I would like to collect my wages so I may go home to my family." The farmer replied, "I have no money for you." So the man said, "Well then, pay me with fruit." And the farmer replied, "I have none." "Then let me have some livestock." "I do not have that either," replied the farmer. "Well have you even any bed linens?" "No," said the farmer. Downcast, the man packed his belongings and went home.

A month later, the farmer took the man's wages and set out for his employee's hometown. When they met, the farmer asked the man, "When you requested your wages and I told you I had no money, what were your thoughts?" The man answered, "I assumed you had just invested all of your capital in a promising business venture." "And when I said I could give you no fruit?" "I assumed it was not yet tithed," said the man. "And what did you think when I said I had no livestock?" the farmer asked. "I assumed that you had rented them all out." "And when I said I had no bed linens?" "I could only assume you had consecrated all that you owned to charity," the man answered. "That is in fact what occurred," said the farmer. "Now, just as you have judged me favorably, so shall you be judged favorably. As I have no children to bequeath my fortune to, I should like to bequeath it to you and your family. And may your compassionate ways be handed down from generation to generation.''

Be compassionate to everyone. Since we are not qualified to judge whether someone is worthy of compassion or not, the only solution is to be compassionate to everyone without regard to whether we think they deserve it. When we see images of starving children in faraway countries, we don't even question whether they deserve our compassion, it is obvious that they do. And at those times, we can be very generous.

But when it is not so obvious, for example, with a convicted bank robber, we can be cruel in our judgment. The problem is that seldom do we know all of the facts to determine whether someone deserves our compassion or not. But if we were to hear his life story, that his mother was a drug addict and that he never even met his father, we begin to see that there are many sides to every story. Of course I am not suggesting that the robber not be punished for his crime, he should be. But we still need to treat him with compassion and kindness. If we had the same history that he did, could we say with absolute certainty that we wouldn't have ended up as a bank robber too? How we judge this person says more about our own character traits than it does about the robber.

In the modern world, we are taught to think the worst of people. If we are walking down a dark street, we immediately suspect the man behind us is a mugger. If we are standing at the automatic bank machine, we think that the person next to us is trying to read our access code. If we misplace something at work, we immediately think the cleaning crew must have taken it during the night. This is our defense mode in action, helping protect ourselves. But there are times when it is necessary to overcome our defensiveness. We must not condemn those around us be-

cause we are protecting ourselves. Rather, we must
give people a chance to prove their trustworthiness.

Andy told me of a time when he was waiting at
the airport for his friend to pick him up. He was
approached by a decent-looking man who said that
his wallet had been stolen and then asked Andy to
lend him twenty dollars. He promised to pay it back
as soon as he reached his final destination. Andy was
torn. He knew people come up with these lines all
of the time, and his own defensiveness wanted to
just say no, but Andy thought, "What if I were in his
situation?" So he gave the man the money figuring if
he didn't get it back, it was his charitable contribution for the month. It is hard to know what to do all
the time, but what is most important here is that
Andy asked himself, "What if I were in his situation?" That is the meaning of compassion.

Be Patient

Patience begins with a detachment from always
having things "your way." For those of us who have
very strong opinions about how everything "should"
be done, this can be extremely difficult! Especially
when "our way" of doing things is far superior to
the way others are doing it! Lillian recounted an
event that forever changed her view of what patience
really means. She decided to volunteer for an organization that had a very tight-knit group that had been
working together for five years. On her first night,
she joined the group in preparing a mailing for an
upcoming event. They were chatting and laughing,
taking twice as long to get the job done. Lillian
shared with me her opinion that if you create a pro-
duction line, where one person folds the letters, one
person stuffs the letters, one person seals the envelopes, and the next person puts the stamp on, it goes
very quickly because you can do your task without
thinking. It is also a lot easier because you can talk

without losing track. And if you get tired or bored, you just swap tasks. At this meeting, everyone had their own stack of letters, envelopes, labels, and stamps. Lillian sat there watching them muddle through the mailing, realizing that at this rate she wouldn't be home until after eleven o'clock. The only problem was, she was the only person at the table who was bothered by this.

After restraining herself for about an hour, the president of the organization went into the kitchen for a soft drink, so Lillian followed her. She said that she had an idea that would make their endeavor more efficient. She shared the idea, certain that everyone would have a much more enjoyable time at the meeting if they stuffed envelopes "her way." The president said that someone had suggested the same idea a year or so back, but no one wanted to try it. Just as Lillian was about to explain to her the benefits of her idea, another group member came up and started talking to the president about something else. Lillian stood there with her soda looking like she was enjoying herself, but inside she wanted to scream. After a few minutes, everyone went back to the dining room table and Lillian followed them without saying a word. For the next hour, she sat at the table, folding twenty letters, stuffing twenty envelopes, and sealing twenty flaps. She didn't talk to anyone, and was at such a boiling point that she couldn't wait for the night to be over so that she could go home with the intention to never volunteer with that group again.

And then something happened. Lillian overheard a conversation between the woman and man next to her. Her son was going through a divorce. The man seemed to know all of the details, but from what Lillian could surmise, there were apparently two children involved, and there was a big court battle going on. The man was divorced himself, and also had two children from his marriage. As they talked, Lillian could almost feel the effects that this man's compassion was having on this woman. It was not just his feelings and thoughts he shared, it was the sympathetic way he listened that made a strong impact. She seemed so raw, so vulnerable, and this man's kindness was soothing and healing to her. Lillian realized that this group's objective was not to be efficient. Their objective was to share their lives with each other. She suddenly realized that her attachment to doing things "her way" had kept her from what she truly found missing in her life: close friends to share her life with.

Impatience is like a downward spiral. The more frustrated we are, the more frustrated we get. At times when we are most annoyed we should develop the habit of just letting go. We will not only live happier lives, but those around us will be happier.

Let's say you are having an argument with your roommate. You are absolutely certain that it is better to tell the landlord about all the things wrong with your apartment while she thinks that you should bring things up one at a time. You argue about it for ten minutes. Letting go would mean saying, "You know what, we've been talking about this for a long time, why don't we think about it for a day or two, and then talk again." All of the fury that each of you may have had and the tensions that were building become completely diffused. Now the two of you can give serious thought to what the other person has said, at your own leisure, and without the pressure of trying to prove that you are right.

Patience means not rushing. Martin had a habit of leaving things for the last minute and then rushing to meet his deadlines. He decided to restructure his life in such a way that he had more time and less rush. We designed a calendar for Martin to schedule his work a few weeks in advance. He decided to give up watching every sports game on television, and limited it to only his favorite teams. He would not answer the phone if it rang while he was on his way out the door to work, and he went to bed earlier so he could wake on time. With a little bit of planning, and a lot of effort, Martin was able to break his frenzied pattern. This gave him the freedom to spend less energy managing his life, and more time to be with people.

Be Forgiving

When someone has wronged us, our first impulse is outrage. It is incomprehensible to us that someone could wrong us and think he/she can get away with it! There was a woman in my class named Mercedes, who had been holding a grudge against another woman for fifteen years. Back in high school there had been four opening spots on the cheerleading squad and Mercedes had practiced all summer long for the fall tryouts. In September, there were two weeks of training followed by three days of "cuts." Mercedes made it through the first two days of cuts, and knew she would make the team because there were now only seven people vying for the four spots. Three of the girls had not practiced all summer, their routines looked clumsy, and one of the girls couldn't even do a split. As it turned out, the girl who couldn't do a split took the spot that should have been given to Mercedes, because her father ran the charity funding the football team. Mercedes was absolutely convinced that he had pulled strings to get his daughter onto the squad.

What bothered Mercedes to this day was not that she didn't make the team, it was the injustice. If Mercedes's supposition is correct, and the father *did* pull strings to get his daughter on the team, she does have a reason to be upset. But holding onto resentment for so many years accomplishes nothing. In fact, it is very unhealthy for Mercedes. Still, to this day, when she sees cheerleaders on television or at a sporting event, an angry feeling comes over her. If she meets someone who looks like her old nemesis, she admits that she often dislikes her on the spot. But the worst part is the energy her resentment wastes! The first important step to forgiveness is to see what significance a certain injustice has played in your life. When Mercedes examined the significance her cheerleading loss made in her life, it seemed infinitesimal compared to the energy she spent in being angry all those years.

Part of the forgiveness process is to recognize the good that comes out of a bad situation. After eleven years, Brad was fired from his job at a large brokerage firm because of a personality conflict with his new boss. He was so angry that he couldn't even drive down the street where the firm was located. If the company had an advertisement on television, he would change the channel. After six months of looking for a job without success, he decided to start his own business of teaching classes on how to manage your finances. He taught the courses all over his city, and eventually was asked to speak in other cities. Because of his experience and personable way of explaining complex issues, he soon had more requests for business than he could fulfill. And, he absolutely loved teaching. It was the most fulfilling job he had ever had. After all of his success, you would think he would thank his lucky stars he was fired. If he hadn't been fired, he would never have ventured out on his own. But Brad still would not drive down the street where his old firm was located. And he often daydreamed about being in front of a large audience with them all applauding, and having one of the people from his old firm sitting in the crowd. When the local newspaper did a story on him, all he could think about was whether the boss who fired him read the article or not. He thought of maybe mailing it to the man anonymously, or having a friend drop it off at the office. Brad was carrying his resentment to an extreme, but it is not that uncommon to bear grudges for a long time. The way to get on the other side of this is to focus on the good that comes out of a situation. Maybe even thinking of it as "fate" helps, but to spend precious energy on holding a grudge robs you of being able to use that energy for fulfilling your potential.

Understand that other people make mistakes and they need your forgiveness. No one is perfect. Many times people are pushed into a corner and have to make decisions that affect us in a negative way, but they may have no other choice. Your role is to forgive those who have wronged you, give up the grudge against them, and *move on*. The ability to be forgiving and compassionate will not only lighten your burden, but will be a great asset when it comes to a relationship with a potential mate. How do you think others will feel about you when they see you forgive someone? Without a doubt they will see you as someone who has a lot of love to offer!

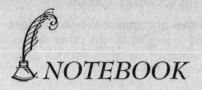

NOTEBOOK

- Write down an incident where someone "wronged" you.

- Now invent a possible explanation for their behavior.

- Are you defensive?

- In what ways can you plan your life to rush less?

- Who in your past have you been unwilling to forgive?

Honesty

Angie really liked Richard. He lived on the same floor of her apartment building. They chatted every time they met in the hall and she enjoyed his company. He was a doctor just starting his own private practice. Smart, handsome, and very kind, Angie secretly fantasized about having a relationship with him, but she was waiting for him to pursue her.

Richard liked Angie as well. She was very friendly, pretty, and had a contagious laugh. He secretly fantasized about dating her, but he was waiting for her to give him a sign that she was interested. He was a little intimidated to ask her out because she was the top stockbroker at her firm, and dressed more glamourously than any woman he had ever met.

Finally, after work one day, Angie and Richard stepped into the elevator together. Angie invited him over to dinner and he accepted. That night their relationship began. Angie told Richard how exciting her work was. She told him about her rise in the company, and about the awards she had won. She told him that she was following in the footsteps of her father who had retired at forty-two as a legend in the industry. Everything about Angie exuded success and gentility. Richard, a man from a modest upbringing, was thrilled to have found such a "great catch" and found himself falling deeper and deeper in love with Angie.

The truth took two months to rise to the surface. Angie's phony airs did not give her away. Her fancy clothes from secondhand shops did not give her away. Even her made-up stories about stock market trades did not give her away. What gave Angie away was a woman in their building who told Richard that Angie was a secretary, not a broker, at a stock-brokerage firm. Why had Angie lied? Because she didn't think a doctor would be interested in dating a "mere" secretary. Why did she embellish the stories including inventing a mogul father? Because she wanted her story to sound realistic.

So now what will happen to the relationship? All of a sudden, Richard realizes that Angie is not the woman that he has fallen in love with. He has been having a relationship with the "image" that Angie is projecting. Now he has to start the relationship all over again. But do you really think that Richard is motivated to learn about who Angie really is now that he cannot trust her? If he is going to have to start a whole new relationship anyway, wouldn't it just be easier for him to start it with a new person who is more trustworthy?

Be Proud of Who You Are

Stop comparing yourself to others. Many of my students tell me that they feel intimidated by people whom they perceive as more accomplished, talented, smarter, or superior to them. It is perfectly natural to feel this way but it can be devastating to one's self-esteem. You must be proud of who you are. No matter what your family background is, what you have accomplished, what experiences you have been through, or how you think you measure up to others, you need to develop a sense of appreciation for who you are as a person.

Recognize that you cannot possibly compare yourself to others accurately. Maybe they have great material wealth, but you might be kinder. Maybe they have traveled extensively, but you may have many more friends. Or maybe they have several postgraduate degrees, but you might have a more practical view of the world. Feeling bad that they are wealthy, world-traveled, or highly educated and you are not is a complete waste of time. You have different strengths and different attributes, and you must stop comparing yourself to others and be proud of who you are.

Comparing yourself to others also leads to boasting, exaggerating, and acting in strange ways to try to impress others. This wreaks havoc on relationships. It is impossible to have an honest relationship with someone based on a phony history or an exaggerated background. Not only will the truth eventually come out, but there is no way for you to feel comfortable with someone when you know that you have not been honest with them. And when they find out that you have not been honest with them, they will not trust you, and will be inclined to leave the relationship.

Tricia, a hairstylist who worked in Hollywood, was a very nice person but she felt like she constantly needed to prove her worth to others. She would try to impress whomever she was talking to by constantly mentioning the famous people who came into her shop. If someone mentioned a new movie release, she would say, "That actress told me that the leading man is a real dreamboat." Or if someone was discussing Italian wines, Tricia would comment, "A famous actor once brought me an Italian scarf." Many times her name-dropping had nothing to do with the conversation, but Tricia's insecurity drove her to drop names whenever she possibly could.

So what is so terrible about Tricia's name-dropping habit? There are two problems with it. First of all, many people would avoid Tricia because they found talking to her tedious and annoying. Even her friends rolled their eyes whenever she dropped a famous name because they were tired of her need to impress them. And secondly, Tricia is robbing herself of the ability to just be herself with others. There is nothing quite so attractive as someone with self-confidence. Anyone can sense right away that Tricia's name-dropping stems from a lack of self-confidence and a need to prove her worthiness. Part of being a great catch is to be proud of who you are, and spend less time comparing yourself in a need to impress others, and more time trying to get to know them.

Keep Your Promises

Jack told Meg that he would call her at 6:00 P.M. He called at 7:00 P.M. Meg didn't care. Jack told Meg that he would get her new wiper blades for her car. He forgot. Meg didn't mind, she got them herself. Jack told Meg he would take her to a fancy restaurant. He then said he couldn't afford it at the moment. Meg didn't mind. They went Dutch treat. Jack told Meg that he would take her to the movies, but he went with friends instead. Meg minded.

Why does it make any difference whether Jack kept his promises or not? Wouldn't it be pretty finicky for us to condemn Jack for calling an hour late? It might be, but when a person has a habit of being undependable, the level of mistrust in the relationship grows. Part of being honest includes keeping your promises. If you want a successful, stable relationship, your mate needs to be able to believe you and depend on you.

When you are honest, then you will attract someone who is also honest. Honesty attracts honesty, and this is one of the most important characteristics in a healthy relationship. How would you feel knowing that your spouse is so honest that he/she couldn't even conceive of ever cheating on you? What would it be like to not doubt your spouse when he says he is working late? Or if he said he was going to pick you up at the airport, you could count on him to be there. Or if she said the bills had been paid, you would know they were. But if you want to marry an honest person, you must be an honest person first.

Get Rid of Those Lying Habits

One of the best ways to become more honest is to get rid of lying habits. The best way to do this is to stop your falsehood mid-sentence. If your boss asks you if you have finished the report, and you respond, "Oh yes, I just need to print it out of the printer which is currently not working," when in truth you have not finished the report, stop yourself mid-sentence, and add the comment, "Um, and plus I have one last page to finish, but it shouldn't take me too long." If your friend asks you if you have finished using her camera, and you respond, "Of course, I will bring it over to your house this weekend," when in truth you have no intention of bringing it by over the weekend, add the comment, "Actually, I could use a few more shots, can I keep it for another week?" Even though she might be annoyed, at least she will know that she can trust you to be straight with her. You will be developing trust and honesty in the relationship.

Remember that telling falsehoods is a habit. Most people are probably very honest at heart, but sometimes telling falsehoods is the path of least resistance. It is just easier. Unfortunately it leads to mistrust and loss of self-esteem. Even recognizing your own falsehoods is a powerful first step. Learning to stop yourself mid-sentence takes time, but every time you are able to do it, you will feel a surge of self-respect.

Getting rid of this habit is a step-by-step process and over time you will be able to see a marked difference. Don't worry if you are not able to correct every falsehood at the beginning; this is a long-term project. Just keep telling yourself you are doing the best you can, and resolve to correct more falsehoods in the future. If you find yourself in the middle of a story that is completely made up, stop yourself midsentence, and if you can't quickly think of a way to rectify the situation, then change the subject completely! The other person probably won't even notice, especially if you ask them a question. Or if you have told someone that you are a black belt in karate, and that someone repeats this to a group of people, you might say, "You know, sometimes I tend to exaggerate." You might feel a twinge of embarrassment at the time, but people will learn to respect your accuracy, and most importantly, you will begin to respect yourself.

Often it will feel like we tell more falsehoods than truths, and seeing these falsehoods can make us feel bad about ourselves. Somehow, it was easier when we were accustomed to falsehoods, and we didn't realize the harm that they do to ourselves and to others. That is why it is so important to acknowledge even the smallest effort that you make to keep from speaking falsehoods. Don't be too hard on yourself. If you accidentally tell a falsehood and can't correct it in time, don't think that you are a bad person. We all make mistakes, and sometimes we make more mistakes when we are focused on something so specifically that we want to be correct. Just resolve to be more accurate next time. But with time, and effort, you will become a person who is more accurate than you might be now, and that is something to be very proud of.

NOTEBOOK

- Do you consider yourself honest? Honestly?

- Have you made up a story about yourself that you now regret relaying?

- Have you been in a relationship where either of you were hurt by a lie or have you hurt someone else with one? How do you feel about that lie today?

- What truths about yourself do you share with potential mates?

Speaking Carefully

Debbie was standing at the water cooler filling a pitcher with water. A man walked up to her and while he waited for her to finish said, "Hey Deb, did you hear Diana got yelled at by Mr. Wicket?" "No kidding, what for?" she asked. "I don't know, but her secretary said that Mr. Wicket stormed out of the room afterwards." Her pitcher full, Debbie nodded in amazement and walked back downstairs to her desk.

Jack stormed into Debbie's office a moment later and threw a stack of papers on her desk. "Debbie, this is not what I wanted at all! What were you thinking of?" Debbie's face reddened. "I expected a lot more from you Deb. I want you to take this upstairs to Diana Green's office and have her review the specifications right away." Without thinking, Debbie blurted out, "She's not exactly the one I should turn to. Mr. Wicket can't stand her, and she's probably on her way out anyway." Jack looked at her in shocked disbelief. "Well go up to Bradley's office then. I needed this twenty minutes ago!" He turned and walked abruptly out of the office.

Jack walked into the executive lounge to get some

coffee and found Joe Applebaum there, eating a danish. "Joe, can I ask you something?" "Sure Jack, what?" "If a senior partner leaves, what's the process for the new selection?" "Oh, I don't know," Joe replied, "it depends on why they left, if they were fired or quit. But I suppose they would review the junior partners to see who is next in line. That person might get promoted prematurely to help with the case load." Just then Diana Green walked into the lounge. Jack nodded to her a little condescendingly. Joe greeted her warmly, but Jack, not wanting to get too close to someone who was on her way out, left. Diana turned to Joe and said, "You know, Mr. Wicket has such a temper. He has been warned by the board many times, but after he blew up this morning, they decided to terminate him."

Gossip. It ruins careers and relationships. Gossip is never okay, and it almost always hurts someone. There is never a time when it won't damage the gossiper, the listener, and the person spoken about. So why does everyone do it? And just because everyone does it, does that make it right? Gossip is so prevalent in society that a person would actually appear "strange" if they didn't participate! So why should we be the good guys? Why should we go out of our way to stop gossiping and even refuse to listen when someone else comes to us with a juicy story?

Mrs. Ames slowly makes her way down the street with her handbag tucked neatly under her arm. She walks by the fruit stand and nods her head to the proprietor. He nods back. A patch of ice covering the width of the sidewalk stops Mrs. Ames in her tracks. She pulls her aging hand out of the glove to grip the side of the building. As she begins to cross the ice, a young man wearing a jeans jacket rushes around the corner and snatches her handbag out of her hand. He roughly pushes her against the brick wall. Mrs. Ames, eighty-seven, is rescued by the fruit store owner, who catches her before she falls to the ground.

It is easy to see that the assailant is guilty of wrongdoing. In fact, most would agree that he deserves a harsh punishment. So why is it difficult for us to see that gossip often does even more damage than stealing or pushing someone? From your own experience, can you honestly say, "Sticks and stones may break my bones, but words will never hurt me?" Haven't we all, at some time in our lives, wept into our pillow about some cruelty inflicted on us by words?

Gossip is the worst use of words. Gossip is any statement, even if not meant in a derogatory way, which might cause mental anguish, physical pain, financial loss, hurt feelings, jealousy, or a damaged reputation. Even if it is said without malice, gossip can do irreparable damage. Gossip breaks up marriages, ruins careers, stops someone from proposing marriage, causes people to mistrust others, and breaks up business partnerships. It doesn't even matter if the gossip is true or not! If someone were to say to your co-worker that the only reason you got your job is because of your looks, that you are not very bright, and that you'll be out the door the minute you slip up, your co-worker is going to lose respect for you and treat you differently. And if she doesn't like you or is competitive with you, she will tell this gossip to others. She will be as guilty of harming you as the man who mugged the elderly woman.

Understand the Motives for Gossip

Gossip makes us feel superior to others. Shelley made the cheerleading squad, but you did not. Yet, you are a history whiz while Shelley gets D's. Why not tell everyone how stupid Shelley is? Conrad drives a Mercedes Benz. He struts around in expensive suits. Can he really afford all of that on his salary? Why not tell everyone, (jokingly of course . . .) that you suspect him of illegal activities? Martha's daughter got straight A's. Yours didn't. Why not share with everyone why Martha's husband left her? The urge to feel superior to others is unfortunately a trait inherent in human beings. Our job is to keep it in check. It starts with being happy with ourselves and with our own accomplishments.

Others gossip to gain power. Recall the example of Mr. Wicket yelling at Diana Green. Every person who learned of this incident tried to use it to his or her advantage. Debbie tried to diffuse Jack's anger by putting Diana down, and Jack saw this as his opportunity to gain the position of senior partner. Gossip spreads through an office faster than most other pieces of information, whether it is true or not. If a new employee joins a firm and is advancing quite rapidly, gossip can derail his entire career. A jealous co-worker might inadvertently mention that the new employee was fired from his last job because of dishonest practices. We all feel perfectly justified in spreading this gossip, as it raises our own level of power as well. But what if that new employee was you? What if you had had plenty of opportunities at your former job to be dishonest, which would have been very profitable for you, but you adamantly refused to be dishonest? How crushing the blow would be to be thought of as dishonest. We never want to be the victim of gossip, but when we spread gossip, we seldom stop to think how the person gossiped about would feel. Most people have been taught to look out for themselves, even if it is at someone else's expense.

Rumor had it that Rob had once embezzled a lot of money from his former company. It was the reason why he was fired and the reason he could not get another job and thus was forced to start his own business. When Gloria met Rob, she had a good feeling that he was a nice and honest person. When she heard the rumors about his past, she was cautious, but having been the victim of ugly rumors herself, she decided not to believe them. In fact, the more she got to know Rob, the more she championed him whenever anyone tried to slander him. She believed in him when no one else would. In time, Gloria discovered that the rumors were not true. Lies had been started by Rob's former co-workers, who were jealous of his rise in his former company. Rob saw Gloria as a woman who would stand by him no matter how bleak the picture looked. He saw her as someone who trusted her own instincts rather than listening to gossip, and someone who was compassionate enough to give him the benefit of the doubt. These are all qualities that he was looking for in a wife, and the two of them eventually got married.

Learn to Recognize Gossip

Many things can constitute gossip: imitating someone's voice or gestures, sarcastic comments or witticisms concealing insults, embarrassing someone for his lack of knowledge or family background, reminding someone of his previous misdeeds, or repeating well-known derogatory information. Any information that seems as if it should be kept secret should not be repeated. Even making an insulting comment and then saying, "I was only joking," is gossip. Even if you do not mention a person's name, but it is discernible who that person might be; this is considered gossip.

People use many excuses to alleviate their blame for gossip such as: "What I said is true," or "I'd say it even if she were here," "Everyone knows it anyway," "He'll never know I said it," "I did the same thing myself," "I wouldn't mind if someone said the same thing about me," or "We're close friends so she won't mind." None of these reasons justify gossip.

Including yourself in the gossip does not sanction it either: "We both misbehaved terribly when we were younger." Even implying that someone has done something wrong without being specific is wrong, "Boy, it's good to see Michael behave so well after all that he's done." Even if the gossip doesn't end up causing damage, we lose our dignity when we participate. There is no difference between volunteering gossip and being pressured into repeating it.

And listening to gossip does just as much damage, as it spurs the gossiper to continue. If you refuse to listen, gossipers cannot spread rumors. Furthermore, if you inadvertently overhear some gossip, you are not obligated to believe it. There are always many sides to every story. Your compassion should go out to the person who is being talked about. And it is best to stay away from people who habitually gossip, as you may be their next victim.

Mollie liked a man named Eddy at her sports club. She timed her arrival at the club to coincide with his every day after work. Eddy thought Mollie was pretty, but he also felt that she had a loose tongue and made way too many sarcastic remarks about other members. Then Eddy met Helen, a new member and a quiet woman. Unknown to Mollie, Eddy and Helen began dating. When Mollie noticed that Eddy was overly solicitous to Helen, she found him alone and told him that though Helen was quiet, she was a very devious woman. Eddy, who by now knew Helen pretty well, knew that Mollie was fabricating her story. He reprimanded Mollie for gossiping, and walked away from her abruptly. Is it any wonder that Mollie could not get anyone at the club interested in her?

Don't confuse gossip with inquiries about someone for specific practical purposes. There are circumstances when it might be necessary to talk about someone. You may be considering someone for a business partnership or considering someone for marriage. You may need to review someone's performance for a raise, point out faulty behavior to your children so that they do not behave in a like manner, or work out interpersonal problems. But in these instances, always be sure not to exaggerate. It is very important, before you make your inquiries, that you tell the person the reason why you are inquiring, that you don't want to gossip but that you want information. It is deceptive to do otherwise. If the other person begins to tell you irrelevant information, thank them for their time and get out of the conversation quickly!

Stop the Gossip Habit

If you find yourself gossiping, stop yourself. If you have a habit of talking about your boss to everyone in your office, and someone says, "Did you see the report that the boss put out?" refrain from ridiculing the boss and say, "Oh I did, but I can't talk right now!" People who are used to sharing gossip with you might be put off at first. If you like, you can even tell them that you are trying to gossip less because you feel that it is damaging to others. Refraining from gossip is one of the most honorable and magnanimous things you can do, and you should be very proud of every effort you make.

If every Friday afternoon the office staff has an extended lunch in the cafeteria, and during these sessions people deride others in the department, leave lunch early. If a few members of your volunteer group always sit at a particular table, mostly to chat about everyone else, sit somewhere else for a change. And if you find that your phone conversations with your best friend are riddled with gossip, you might try to sway the conversation to other topics.

If someone starts to gossip with you, stop him/her mid-sentence. Ask them if what is about to be said has a practical benefit. If not, change the subject completely. The gossiper will likely feel bad for a moment, as he/she is used to getting high praise for a juicy bit of gossip, so don't prolong the discomfort. Talk about the latest movie, or compliment his/her clothing.

Gossip is so prevalent in all our daily conversations, and because it is socially acceptable, it makes people uncomfortable when we won't gossip, and we feel like we are fish swimming upstream. That is why it is so important that we constantly acknowledge ourselves for every victory, no matter how small. Joyce, a student in my seminar, told me that she became best friends with Tracy because Tracy refrained from gossiping about her. Joyce was the new kid in town, and everyone was talking about how ridiculous her clothing styles were. Tracy didn't join in their gossiping, and in fact said, "How would you like it if you went to a strange town and didn't know what to wear and everyone made fun of you?" Joyce heard it, extended her hand in friendship, and eventually was maid of honor at Tracy's wedding.

By refraining from gossip, you will have a sense of dignity and pride that no one can take away from you. You will know that you are doing the right thing, and others will know it too. You will give others the impression that you are content with your life and that you don't have to deride others to feel good about yourself. You will be seen as someone who is not malicious or jealous, and compassionate enough not to judge others. This self-confidence is very attractive to people and will certainly not go unnoticed by people who might be interested in you as a mate.

NOTEBOOK

- Do you gossip? Why?

- How can you stop yourself and others from gossiping?

- Your boyfriend tells you an incredible story about your best friend. How can you stop him from spreading a rumor without causing an argument or hurting his feelings?

Humility

The lines at international customs were extraordinarily long during the holiday weekend. The airport bustled with activity and the noise of the overhead paging system added to the fray. A woman arriving from London had an Italian leather valise with a shoulder strap over one shoulder. On the other, an expensive Parisian handbag swung heavily at her side. She stood in a long line that did not seem to be moving. Her hair was rumpled from sleeping on the plane, and her expensive linen pants suit was covered with crease lines. Her angry face belied the elegance that she was attempting to project, and she kept shifting her weight from one foot to the other.

A gentleman wearing a tan uniform and a security badge was walking past her briskly and she stopped him. "Excuse me sir." He turned to look at her. "Yes?" "Um, sir, is there a shorter line that I might go through to get out of here more quickly?" The man smiled, "I'm sure that is what everyone would like to know!" "Sir, I have to be on the set in less than an hour. Do you know who I am?" The man looked at her in confusion and the people on line

turned their heads to try to get a look at the woman
as well. The uniformed man then replied, "I don't
know who you are, but I do know where you are—
in line at international customs where we take care
of everybody—one person at a time." He turned and
walked toward his destination.

The woman was furious! Just then a woman ran
up to her and said, "Oh Miss Flynn! I have not
missed an episode in two years! Please, can I have
your autograph?" The actress was handed a pen and
a small notebook, and she signed her autograph as
those around them looked on. "Oh thank you, thank
you. Wait till my friends see this!" The fan rushed
back to her place in line. Filled with a renewed sense
of deserving special treatment, Miss Flynn asked the
woman behind her to hold her place in line. She went
to the airline worker in front of the line, who looked
up from examining an opened suitcase. "Yes?" "Excuse me, my name is Sondra Flynn, and I would like
to go through right now as I cannot be late to the
television studio. I am the star of the show." The
woman, who continued to examine the suitcase,
looked at her again with no sign of recognition. "I
am not authorized to do that." "Well, who is?" she
asked with exasperation. The woman nodded her
head across the way to the office.

As she walked to the office, all eyes watched her,
some recognizing her face, and others preparing to
be angry if she was allowed to cut ahead in line. The
actress held her head high, feeling quite superior to
those around her. In the office, there was a man at
the counter speaking to the manager, and four men
in dark suits standing on the inside of the doorway
waiting for him. They surveyed her carefully as she
walked into the small room. The man at the desk
was saying to the manager, "Please, sir, I beg of you,
it is not necessary." It was obvious to her that he
was in some kind of trouble. Seeing the fiery look on
the actress's face, the man cordially stepped aside to

let her approach the customs manager. She nodded her appreciation for his recognition of her status, and began speaking to the manager in a condescendingly sweet tone. "Sir, thank you for your time. I am Sondra Flynn. I am the star of a famous television show. I must be on the set in less than an hour and I absolutely cannot wait in line for two hours like everyone else." The manager nodded his understanding and pulled out a special form which he began to fill out. The actress smiled as the manager handed her the form. The actress signed with a fancy, well-practiced script. "Okay if you will just wait here, it will only take a few moments." She thanked him, and finally satisfied, she sat in the one chair in the room. The manager handed the special form to the clerk who went to the side office to process it.

The manager turned his attention back to the man who had been waiting patiently. "Sir, we don't want any trouble getting into the city. Please let us handle it." The actress listened with intrigue. The man shook his head back and forth, "I appreciate your concern, but our parcels are delicate and we would like to handle them ourselves. We would just like to be treated like everyone else." The actress was watching his gentle arm gestures as he pleaded his case. All he wanted was to be treated as well as those poor souls waiting for two hours on line! She thought that maybe she should use her clout to help this poor immigrant, but the clerk called out her name. "Miss Flynn, take this and go to the head of the line up there." She walked proudly to the desk to retrieve her form. *It's lucky to be important,* she thought as she decided that she really didn't have time to help him out. As she left the counter, she overheard the manager as he spoke softly to the man. "Please, Your Highness, I implore you. Let us take you in the helicopter. We promise no fanfare and we will bring your parcels directly to your suites with diligence and with care."

What makes some people arrogant and others humble beyond measure? It might be the personality that we are born with, or how we are raised by our families. But there are also many factors in our culture that foster arrogance. We are taught to think of ourselves first. We are taught to treat others as "things" to be manipulated to our advantage. We are taught to feel superior to others. Movies portray successful moguls as extremely arrogant, as if it is that trait that made them successful. (Is it any wonder teenagers try to emulate the trait of arrogance?) Would you want to marry an arrogant person? The more arrogant a person is, the more difficult it is for him or her to build close relationships. No one wants to befriend someone who treats others in a condescending manner or who makes disparaging remarks.

Humble people, on the other hand, draw people to them like a magnet. They are empathetic with others and look for ways to help them. They are kind and thoughtful, and listen to other people's problems. They are not preoccupied with themselves. Many people erroneously believe that humble people have low self-esteem and that is why they don't try to dominate others. But in fact, you would have to have very high self-esteem to care about others, to be compassionate, and to have the strength to refrain from the natural inclination to dominate others. It is usually low self-esteem that causes a person to become arrogant.

Understanding Arrogance

Arrogant people use their feelings of superiority to put others down and to maintain their own self-images. They put on an air of superiority wherever they go: the grocer, the office, even a close friend's home. And they can never find friends or mates who measure up to their own high levels. As far as they're concerned, everyone is beneath them, and they are continually frustrated that they are unable to get close to people. When they do start knowing someone, they become disgusted by the other person's faults very quickly. They are unable to take the good with the bad because they cannot tolerate bad. And associating with anyone or anything less than perfect punctures their fragile self-image. Ultimately, arrogance stops people from seeing the essential humanity of others.

It is often difficult for arrogant people to admit that someone is good enough for them unless one has all the right "status symbols" to show wealth, power, position, and popularity. Without these symbols, they are unwilling to admit that someone is as good as they are. If someone they consider "faulty" were to be associated with them, it would diminish their stature, something they protect with every ounce of energy they can muster. Arrogant people are unable to appreciate quality individuals because the only qualities they recognize are superficial: how stylishly you dress, which expensive clubs you belong to, and what important people you know.

Arrogant people are unable to muster compassion for others they consider not worthy of their time. They may go through the motions of performing charity work as a way of parading their "goodness" in the eyes of others. Arrogant people have built their entire identities around thinking they are better than others. Humble people, on the other hand, have built their identities on how their actions affect others positively.

I was speaking with Gina in a private session. She wanted to jump-start her plan to "Get Married Now." She told me that she would never admit this to anyone, but she was very upset about not being married yet. It didn't seem fair that people who didn't even have as much to offer as she did were already married. She considered herself the ideal wife. She was fun to be with, ivy-league educated, liked to travel, had her own successful printing company, and was very active in the community. Determined to get married within the year, she wanted me to help her overcome any obstacles in her way. We spent some time going over her past patterns in relationships, and what became obvious right away was Gina's feeling that she kept picking one "loser" after another. The men she described did not sound like bad choices to me and she recounted several stories.

Gina met Barry on the phone. They talked for over three hours and Barry seemed to be the ideal mate for her, so she arranged to meet him in person the following weekend. Gina said to me, "I had never been so excited to meet someone in my whole life. He was smart and cultured, and had a wonderful sense of humor. But I just about died when I met him. He was about fifty pounds overweight and bald! Why do these things always happen to me?!" She told me about another date that she had been on. "This guy was so sweet and kind, but I just couldn't picture myself married to him. For one thing, he was only an inch taller than me, and for another, he didn't even know who Virginia Woolf was. Not to mention the fact that I could never marry someone who hadn't traveled out of the country at least once in his life!"

Finally she told me about a man who she became engaged to. His name was Marcus and he was an airline pilot. They seemed to have the same values when they were alone together, but every time they went to a party or an event together, Gina felt embarrassed to be with him. It's not that he wasn't good-looking, he was quite handsome, but he would always say or do something that really bothered Gina. For instance, once they were at a dinner party and he had four helpings of the lasagna. He slowed down the whole meal for everyone and made a spectacle of himself. The other guests found it amusing, and

Marcus thought it a great compliment to the host, but Gina was mortified.

Another time they were in a restaurant and Marcus was handed the wine list. In front of Gina's best client Marcus said, "I don't really know very much about wines, why doesn't someone else choose a bottle." Gina said it took her over a week to get over that embarrassing comment. But the last straw was when Gina and Marcus were at a friend's wedding. Marcus joined some people on the dance floor performing circuslike stunts to amuse everyone. Marcus walked on his hands, used a napkin like a veil, and pranced around like a drunken bride. Gina said, "I stood hidden behind the crowd watching him and thought to myself, 'I cannot marry this man.' We broke up less than a month later."

I told Gina that she needed to find a husband who met her needs, not her expectations. Whether someone is tall or short, fat, bald, world-traveled, or behaves the way we want them to in public has very little to do with our long-term happiness. Gina is spending too much time judging her dates' superficial qualities and not enough time judging their characters. I have many students who want to marry someone who "looks good" to others, but they put this desire before every other qualification. What is most important is finding someone who meets your needs. I advised Gina to make a list of what she needed to be happy. To concentrate on qualities like honesty, trustworthiness, communication, or thoughtfulness. We discussed what kind of attributes would truly make her happy, but no matter what I said, Gina would not listen to me. She said that she not only wanted all of the great character traits, but she wanted her husband to be rich, handsome, and educated too. She had a lot to offer, and deserved someone who had it all.

Gina told me that her mother's friends all said she was "unmarriageable" because she was too much of

a go-getter and too picky. Being a "go-getter" was
not the problem. One should feel proud of one's accomplishments, and the more you go after your goals
and succeed, the prouder you should be. It is when
people make the leap to thinking that these accomplishments make them better than others that arrogance sets in. And it's fine to be picky, as long as
you're picky about the right things. Gina is spending
too much time looking for superficial qualities. She
is looking for someone who fits her ideal "picture"
and who looks good on paper. But when someone
looks good on paper, we may overlook some serious
character flaws that might lead to unhappiness for
the rest of our lives. Gina told me that all of her
friends from college married "great catches," and she
was even better looking than they are! So she told
me that she was not willing to settle for anything
less than they had.

I asked her if she really knew about her friends'
husbands at all. She proceeded to give me a listing
of occupations: stockbroker, accountant, doctor, man-
ufacturer, etc. I asked her if these men, with all their
"success symbols," dedicated time to helping others
less fortunate than themselves, or did they selfishly
just enjoy the fruits of their "superiority"? But Gina
didn't know. The only times she saw these men were
when they went out to restaurants in a group. She
told me they seemed fabulous. But what did she really know? Maybe they were on their best behavior
when Gina saw them but at home they were verbally
and emotionally abusive. Maybe behind a friend's
smiling face is a deep grief that she has married for
"looking good on paper" and was now paying the
price with her happiness. Maybe some of her friends
are about to get divorced. Gina would have no way
of discerning any of this.

If, in her arrogance, Gina proceeds to look for a
husband that fits her picture of a "great catch," she
will be destined to find someone who will not make

her happy. The reason is that you can either focus your search on your "pictures" or your needs, and the two are mutually exclusive. Gina was more attached to the "pictures" of what she was looking for than interested in finding someone who would truly make her happy. I don't blame Gina for feeling the way she does. Many of my students who have all of the "symbols" of success often have a difficult time finding a mate. Society has taught them that they are what they have accomplished. Their success is their identity. Unfortunately, this way of measuring people's identity leads to arrogance. If success is identity, the next thought that follows is that someone with more success is better than someone with less. And this arrogance makes it hard for us to be close to people—because no one can be on our level if we want to continue feeling superior to everyone.

Be aware that arrogance can cost you your happiness. If single people would only look for mates based on what they need to be happy, they would see that the appropriate mate for them is not someone who has "symbols" that match theirs, rather it is someone who has the character traits that will make them happy for the rest of their lives. What do you think it would feel like to have a mate who is totally honest with you? When he said he loved you and would do everything in his power to stay with you forever, you would know he meant it. What would it feel like to have someone who cared more about your broken-down car than his own errands? What would your life be like if you knew, with absolute certainty, that your husband would never be unfaithful to you? The moment arrogance loosens its grip on us, we are able to see what is truly important. We are able to find someone of true quality, a real "great catch."

Clorese, a Get Married Now™ seminar participant, had been married for four years and later divorced. She very much wanted to remarry and have children, but she was having a very difficult time finding a husband who was accepted by her social circle. She told me that all of her friends said she had "married beneath her" the first time around, and that is why it ended in divorce. Her friends disapproved of every man she considered dating. I told her that the phrase "marrying beneath you" is used by people who think that humans can be graded like cartons of eggs. Depending on how many success "symbols" they have, one can judge their quality. However, it has about as much depth and insight into human character as rating eggs. Clorese needs to stop focusing on the superficial aspects of her search, and realize that her feelings of superiority stop her from finding the right mate. Clorese needs to get a clear picture of what she needs to make her happy. She should make a top-ten list of those needs, and then find someone who matches that list. She needs to forget about what her friends say, and about the superficial symbols that have nothing to do with long-term happiness. It is far more important to have strong character traits that meet your needs than it is to have superficial symbols.

Being Humble

Knowing how to show appreciation is one of the best qualities you can have—and humble people know how to be grateful. Even with all of life's difficulties, there is always much to be grateful for: being alive, having our health, having people who care for us, not starving to death, having a job, having a nice pair of shoes, being close to a convenience store, being able to read, having good character traits, and much more. Most of the time we don't stop to think about it. We are so absorbed in our daily affairs, or so busy going from one crisis situation to the next, that gratitude is the last thing we even think about. Maybe if we hear of another's hardship, or when we go to a funeral and realize that one day we, too, will be dust, we stop and think about how much we are grateful for. It is only when our feeling of gratefulness translates into taking action, into doing a kind deed for someone else, that we are showing our appreciation maximally.

Being humble means thinking of others. This is the antithesis of arrogance. Whereas arrogance leads to speaking disparagingly about others, humility will cause someone to be extremely careful about other people's feelings. Arrogance drives people away because no one likes to be treated poorly; humility brings people closer because everyone likes to be treated well. Arrogance causes one to be wrapped up in oneself, humility gives us the opportunity to stop focusing on ourselves all the time. Thinking of oneself all of the time becomes tedious. Self-absorption and constantly dissecting one's own problems lead to low self-esteem and the sense that we must "fix" ourselves. But thinking of others is the exact way to get us out of this downward spiral that is created by thinking only of ourselves. Do something nice for someone. Go visit someone in the hospital. Speak favorably about someone. Protect the dignity of others by not listening to gossip about them. Take out the trash when it really isn't your turn. And even when you are having a major crisis at work and your friend rambles on about what outfit you think she should wear on her next date, give her all of the time she needs before starting in with your problems.

Cultivating Humility

First, stop boasting. Some people boast more than others, but when students ask me the quickest way to becoming less arrogant, I recommend they pay close attention to their boasting habits, and do what they can to boast less. Unfortunately, boasting is not discouraged in our society. People flaunt their wealth with unrestrained vanity. People tout their accomplishments without regard to those listening. And it is considered perfectly polite conversation to brag about one's family origins or about all the famous people one knows. In this atmosphere, it is difficult to withstand the urge to play the game of one-upmanship. It is also difficult to imagine being the only person in a conversation not to boast. But it is possible. And your restraint will help others to give up the game and begin relating to one another as people instead of trying to outdo one another.

Although at a job interview, boasting is likely to land you the job, in most instances boasting only has one result: to alienate others. But if we begin to study our boasting habits, we will see that after we boast, we don't feel any closer to the people we are talking to. We don't even feel superior really. We know that we have relied on completely superficial qualities to impress others. Did we boast to feel better than others? To make others feel inferior to us? To win some power over them? Maybe we just wanted a pat on the back? Sometimes boasting must be limited to family and friends, the people with whom you also share your failures and troubles. Stopping yourself from boasting mid-sentence takes great strength of will, but the results will be instantaneous. You will feel better about yourself, and you will be free of the enormous burden of constantly needing to impress others! This will do more for your self-image than being best friends with the president!

My student Gail told me that she went over to someone's house for a meeting and was absolutely overwhelmed with the magnitude of the home. The marble foyer was larger than her own living room, the kitchen was larger than her whole apartment, and the artwork displayed was more beautiful than anything she had ever seen. And the woman who lived there was her own age! Gail could not stop thinking about that home for months. It is understandable that she felt jealous of such wealth, but Gail should ask: Was the woman who owned the house kind? Did she flaunt her wealth, making everyone else feel worthless? Or did she humbly say how fortunate she felt to be able to have a home like this? Did she gossip for the duration of the meeting? Was she compassionate to those less fortunate? Was she an honest, down-to-earth person? These are the important values that we need to aspire to. Everyone wants great wealth, but sometimes great wealth can obscure our ability to attain true greatness of character. Gail is extremely kind and should be very proud and very happy about who she is—she should not compare herself to this other woman.

When we replace arrogance with humility, we feel good about ourselves and do not need to prove our worth by feeling superior to others. If someone asks us if we were successful in college, we don't need to say, "I would say so, I graduated magna cum laude." We might instead joke, "Of course, I was the ping-pong champion of my dorm!" If someone is walking around the office boasting of their new twenty-foot boat, and feeling quite superior to everyone else, there is no need to tell them that you spent every summer on your uncle's seventy-foot yacht. If we walk into a restaurant and spot a woman in a rumpled coat waiting for a table, and our natural inclination is to feel superior to her, we need to think instead, "I don't even know this person, how can I deem to feel superior to her?" Maybe she is a brain surgeon who doesn't care about appearances. Thinking this way will make us less inclined to feel superior and arrogant toward others.

Being humble in an arrogant world is difficult. It takes time. And it takes effort to continue to be humble. You should be very proud of every single time you replace an arrogant sentence with one that is more humble. Every time you think of another instead of just yourself, you should acknowledge it.

Even if you spend an entire evening playing one-upmanship at a dinner party, don't berate yourself too harshly. In the growth process there is always some movement forward and some movement backward. Just try to be more humble in the future. And don't fall into the trap of feeling self-righteous about how humble you are. Don't berate others for being arrogant. Either the pull to be arrogant in this environment is too strong, or they simply don't know better. Maybe your example will help them to change. But remember, as the quality of humility grows in your life, your sense of self and your self-esteem will grow by leaps and bounds. You will attract more people of quality to you, people will like you more, and you will feel closer in your relationships than you may have ever thought possible.

NOTEBOOK

- Write down your top-ten list of what you *need* in a mate.

- In what ways do you feel superior to others?

- What are you grateful for in your life?

- How does thinking of others help you to be humble?

- What is most difficult about trying to stop boasting?

- How can being humble keep peace within a relationship?

Part Four

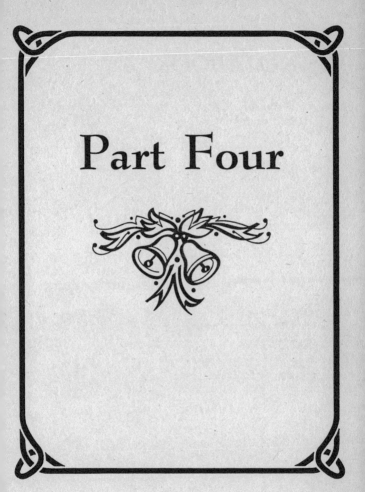

EMPOWERING OTHERS

Much of what this book has focused on so far is teaching you how to fulfill your potential as a human being in order to be a great catch. Hopefully by now, you have some powerful insights into yourself, as well as very clear guidelines as to how to become the kind of person you would like to be. But there is a problem. Working on ourselves, as important as it is, and as valuable as it is, can lead to self-absorption. And unfortunately, self-absorption always leads to an unbalanced, unhappy life. Very fortunately, there *is* a way to combat self-absorption: focus on empowering others.

Empowering others means giving strength and support to another. All of our energy is focused on ourselves. We are thinking about being late to a meeting, worried about how we look, wondering whether we should trade in the old car, concerned about going to the dentist that afternoon, and on and on. But you can step outside your concerns to help another. You drive your friend to pick up her car from being towed. A sister takes you to the airport. Your mother calls to find out how your job interview went. We care about each other, and what's more, we show it. What focusing on empowering others means is that we care more and we show it in more ways.

The first step is to accept yourself. Stop measuring yourself against perfection and recognize that you are fine the way you are. The second step is to accept others. Rather than pick someone apart for every little flaw, try to appreciate him for his strengths. The third step is to learn how to get along with others in an empowering way, and the fourth step is to see what it really takes to support others. The fifth step is to let others support us. By the time you finish this section, you will know exactly how to empower others in a way that will make you a great catch and an even greater spouse!

Self-Acceptance

Charlene came up to me after a lecture one evening and said, "I have been ready to get married for at least four years and haven't been able to find anyone. I really feel like something must be wrong with me." The moment our life doesn't look the way we think it should, we blame ourselves. Recognizing that we have the power to change our future gives us power, but when our future doesn't go the way we want, feeling bad about ourselves is self-destructive. The secret is to chalk up setbacks to the natural way of the world, to acknowledge yourself for trying, and to accept yourself, flaws and all. This will not only make your life more peaceful, but you can also empower others by acting as a role model.

Get Past Inner Turmoil

First, get past your inner turmoil by realizing that there is nothing wrong with you. The fact is, just about everyone feels like something is wrong with them. It seems to be the natural way to feel. Part of self-acceptance is to recognize your weaknesses, and to acknowledge your strengths. If an incident occurs and you handle it awkwardly, so what? If you don't have as many material possessions as your friends, that doesn't mean something is wrong with you. Maybe you haven't established yourself in your career yet. Maybe you have qualities and character traits that they don't have. It does not give you license to put yourself down and to feel like a failure.

Since all of Linda's friends were married, she often felt like the third wheel whenever she visited their homes. Frustrated, she often decided to stay home on Saturday nights. This turned into a worse habit whereupon waking on Saturday morning, she would not take off her bathrobe and she would spend the whole day feeling sorry for herself. She felt like an outcast, as if there was something wrong with her because she couldn't find a husband. But Linda needed to see that her biggest problem was feeling lonely, which is a perfectly natural feeling. But instead of sulking about it, Linda should have been going out and making new friends.

Do not make the mistake of thinking that you need to feel whole and complete in order to be married. It is important to recognize that because marriage is so emotionally fulfilling, and because it can allow us to reach our maximum potential, many people do not feel complete *until* they are married. This is not because they are not healthy, it is because marriage provides support and security that cannot be gained in any other way. So the next time you start thinking, "There's something wrong with me," answer yourself, "No there isn't," and get on with more enjoyable activities.

So many of my students tell me that they don't feel deserving of finding someone of quality. Either they don't feel like a person of quality themselves, they've been through enormous traumas, or they come from dysfunctional families. People who feel unworthy end up settling for a relationship with whomever happens to be in their path, without discriminating whether that person will make them happy. But by now, from reading this book, you should recognize that being a person of quality isn't judged by where you've come from, but by who you are today. Are you kind, do you work toward reaching your potential by bettering your character? Feeling worthy is a gift only you can give to yourself by accepting who you are.

Another way to get past inner turmoil is to stop feeling too set in your ways. The older we get, the more set in our ways we become. Part of this phenomenon is due to maturity and an understanding of what makes us happy and comfortable. This same phenomenon can keep us from having the life we want to have.

You may be used to relaxing at home after work, and if you meet someone who likes to be active in the community every night, you immediately disregard him as a candidate for marriage. Or you are used to a certain comfortable lifestyle and want to maintain it. Then you meet someone who is warm and thoughtful, and meets many of your needs, but when you go to his or her apartment, you see that he or she does not live up to your standards. So you keep your lifestyle at the expense of a future with someone who might possibly have made you happier than you have ever been. Or, you have always dated intellectual people, so when you meet someone who doesn't understand all the classical allusions you make, you feel superior and push her away. Had you spent the time to get to know that person better, you might have been able to see that she was the most honest person you had ever met, or she would have made the best mother in the world. But those people you discarded are gone, and you can now be free to chat on the phone with your friends about what bores they all were.

Being set in our ways keeps us from seeing any

possibility of a relationship other than what we already picture in our heads. The problem is, the person we end up with will never fit our pictures, so sticking to our picture guarantees that we will never find someone. The only way around this is to get rid of your preconceived pictures and be open to a relationship that previously you would never have given a second chance. Then use your top-ten list of what you need to be happy, and see if the person matches that list.

Many people have a picture of what they are looking for based on an amalgamation of the good qualities of every person they have ever dated. Unfortunately, that person does not exist. Taking the bad with the good is hard. Maybe a potential partner is kind, honest, loyal, and caring, but doesn't communicate to the level that you feel you need to be happy. But rather than just dismiss this person, think about the fact that this person has most of what you need, maybe his or her communication level is really a challenge for your own growth. Maybe you need to develop skills in drawing this person out that will be valuable in fulfilling your potential in your own life. Don't be so quick to let someone go who meets many of your needs merely because you assess them as not having everything. There is no person on the planet who will fulfill all of your needs. Maybe whatever is lacking in them is the perfect complement to an area that you need to grow in yourself.

Be Who You Are

To accept yourself you must be able to live with your flaws. Cathy told me that she had a terrible temper. No matter how she tried, when she got angry, she would turn from a rational, kind person into a raving lunatic. She had tried all the methods: counting to ten, walking out of the room, even writing down her thoughts instead of yelling at someone.

None of the methods had worked, and after every raging tantrum, she would sulk for the rest of the day, feeling very bad about herself. It is understandable that Cathy is upset about this issue. It is very frustrating to work toward a goal and not accomplish it. But Cathy needs to realize that she is not perfect. Rather than focusing on her own weaknesses, she should sit down and make a list of all her strengths. For instance, she is very patient with young children, she is very helpful to her family members, she is charitable, friendly, and listens to her friends' problems. And, she works at trying to improve her character traits, including her temper. Part of self-acceptance is to stop being so hard on yourself. Focus on your strengths and stop obsessing over your flaws. The more Cathy worries about her tantrums, and the more she makes herself feel miserable when she has a tantrum, the more the problem will persist. Living with your flaws means that you do what you can to grow out of them. But don't berate yourself needlessly when you are not always productive. If Cathy simply acknowledges that she has a problem with her temper, and then says to herself, "I am going to do the best I can and slowly but surely I will succeed," she would take the pressure off herself and allow her persistent efforts to work their natural course. Thinking of flaws as challenges rather than problems allows us to work on them without feeling bad, and without emotional trauma.

Learn to accept yourself by getting rid of "shoulds." Many people make decisions based on what they think they *should* do without thinking about the issues involved. For instance, a person is offered two jobs at vastly different salaries. He takes the higher paying one because that is what he "should" do. But if he had thought about it thoroughly, he would have realized that the lower paying job might have higher chances for advancement. Or a person decides to purchase the lower priced car because that is what he "should" do. But the higher priced car gets more miles to the gallon and lasts an average of two years longer, with fewer repairs. Or a woman is dating two men and chooses the financially successful one to have a long-term relationship with because that is what she "should" do, never mind that the struggling man has a much stronger character and would make the woman happier.

Sometimes "shoulds" make us barrel ahead without really thinking about what we need or want. A woman in her mid-forties was working very hard to buy herself a condo. She worked close to sixty hours a week toward this goal because she thought that a woman of her age "should" own property. Someone may feel that since all of her friends are married, she "should" be married too. So rather than thinking about what she truly needs to be happy, and searching for a mate based on whether the person matched those needs, she becomes much less discriminating in order to do what she "should" do. The best way to get rid of "shoulds" is to make a list of all the things that you are doing in your life right now because you feel you "should." Then make another list of all of the things that you are doing because you want to be doing them. This will give you clarity as to how to separate the two, but the most important factor is that when you are about to make a decision in your life, ask yourself, "Am I doing this because I think I 'should,' or because it is the right decision to make?"

Feel good about feeling powerful. Many of my female students feel that their success and power are the reasons that they aren't married. They feel that men want weak, subordinate women. This is not true. Being powerful means that you are able to manage your affairs in an efficient, clever way, you are able to stand up for what you believe in without fear of expressing your own opinions, and you handle business situations productively. Power is a very valuable asset. However, power used to step on others to get what you want, feel superior to others, or assert your will over others, is not attractive to anyone. This kind of power most certainly would push people away, men included. Being who you are means allowing your strengths to flourish, and expressing yourself fully. If this is mixed with your desire to be kind, to be compassionate, and to be humble, then you will most certainly attract the kind of person with healthy self-esteem who is appreciative of your power.

Stop Belittling Habits

One way to stop those habits of belittling yourself is by not seeking approval from others. Not only is this constantly exhausting to yourself and others, but it does great damage to your self-esteem. It is fine to get your friends' opinions about things, and it is the mark of someone with strong self-esteem who is willing to listen to opinions other than his or her own. But getting opinions is different from seeking approval. Seeking approval is when you need to get reassurance for every little step you make. It is belittling to yourself. Self-acceptance means that you accept yourself, your opinions, and your decisions.

Marianne seemed to "have it all together." She had a great apartment, a great job, and a great boyfriend. But she constantly needed reassurance about her choices. Not only about the big decisions in her life, but even small items. She would call a girlfriend to seek approval on the outfit she had chosen to wear to a particular event. She would seek approval from her mother on decisions that she made at work, and she would consult her married sister for approval on how she should proceed with her boyfriend. Marianne was never satisfied until someone told her, "You did the right thing," or "You made a good choice." It is fine to have a supportive network, but it is also important to feel good about yourself and to feel confident in your own decisions. What Marianne needs to do is to get out of the habit of phoning people every time she makes a decision. She needs to literally stop herself from calling them. And when she has made a few decisions on her own, her confidence will grow, and she will see that seeking approval for everything is keeping her from feeling fully in charge of her own life.

It is important that we look at our weaknesses in order to work on them and improve ourselves. But many times, people ask for opinions about themselves solely for getting attention. It is a very tempting habit to fall into. After all, we are all our own favorite subject, maybe second only to telling people how they should run their lives! So it is very easy to get another person hooked into a conversation about our weaknesses so others can tell us how to run our lives. However, when the conversation is over, the person, who is likely not a trained therapist, may have told you all kinds of erroneous and possibly damaging information. If your intent is to improve yourself, this information surely will not assist you. And if it is just an exercise in attention-getting, then you will have belittled yourself in that person's eyes. This is not good for your self-esteem. If you want to be analyzed to improve yourself, you should be very proud of yourself. That is a great step toward reaching your potential. Just make sure to do it with someone who is a trained therapist or a very close friend who is as committed to your improvement and your self-esteem as you are.

Another way to stop belittling habits is to stop invalidating yourself. Ron second-guessed everything he ever said to anyone. After he had a meeting with his boss, he would berate himself for not remembering to mention the national sales figures. After a date, he would get mad at himself for not having taken the woman to a nicer restaurant. He was also an avid sports fan and he would berate himself for not having bet on the winning teams. Ron lived in a constant state of regret. Of course, he did not feel good about himself. He bit his fingernails and had nervous stomach spasms. He worried over every little thing. But Ron's problem is not that he never does or says the right thing, it is that he has a constant habit of invalidating himself.

The habit of invalidating oneself is easy to identify. If you constantly think back to events and berate yourself for how you acted, this is invalidating yourself. The most powerful way to stop this habit is to make the commitment to yourself that from now on you will not invalidate yourself. And when you find yourself nullifying something you already stated, empower yourself by saying, "I am not going to invalidate myself. I did the best I could, and no one could ever ask more of me." Or you can say, "It's pointless to brood about this and it's too late to do anything about it now. Next time I'll do better." Since you are in the habit of constantly rehashing an issue, it is likely that you will keep thinking about it, but you must again say to yourself, "I am not going to invalidate myself. I did the best I could at the time." Do whatever you can to distract yourself from thinking about it, and in time, the habit of invalidating yourself will be supplanted by the habit of empowering yourself!

NOTEBOOK

- What makes you feel unworthy?

- How are you set in your ways?

- What flaws have you been unwilling to live with that you would be willing to live with now?

- Make a list of the "shoulds" that have ruled your life and then make another list of the things that would make you happy.

- Do you seek approval from others?

Accepting Others

Very often we do not let people just be who they are. We either reject them or try to change them into who we want them to be. But the ultimate challenge is to accept them exactly as they are. This not only gives them the freedom of full self-expression, but it also frees us of the burden of thinking of a way to change them all the time. Wouldn't you much rather spend your time with a friend who just lets you be yourself, rather than with someone who is constantly suggesting ways to improve yourself? Once we learn to accept others, flaws and all, we learn to care about them; this is a much more fulfilling way to live. You should accept the stranger standing in front of you at the post office as well as the people with whom you spend time: co-workers, acquaintances, friends, and family. Accepting others means to stop judging them and to start learning about them. Part of being a great catch is appreciating your mate exactly as he/she is.

Don't Judge Quickly

Don't rely on first impressions. It is unfair to size people up in a minute, and then interact with them

179

as if you know them. This robs you of finding out who they really are and what they are like. Not only might you never learn valuable information about that particular person, but you will forego the opportunity of developing the skill of accurately assessing another person's traits.

The expression, "You never have a second chance to make a good first impression," is true. But what is far more important than a first impression is what the person turns out to be like when you have known them for a while. We have all met people who have made fabulous first impressions, but then turned out to be very unlikeable. It would make much more sense for people to forego their initial impressions in exchange for discerning what a person is like over time. When you are interacting with people, don't get caught up in the trap of judging by first impressions. You will either end up having the wool pulled over your eyes, or you will dismiss someone who might have wonderful qualities merely because they are not adept at making good first impressions.

Learn to recognize your prejudices. We all have prejudices, regardless of our education or intelligence. If we are poor, we may dislike rich people, if we are rich we may dislike poor people. If we are thin, we may look down upon heavy people. If we are educated we may dislike people without an education. If we are attractive we may not want to associate with people who are not as attractive. We may not like people of a particular country, or from our neighboring town. We may be prejudiced against a particular race or religion, or we may not like to talk to people who can't speak our language. Whatever the case, for some reason, humans have the habit of polarizing into groups and disliking other groups. This is unfortunate, and the only way to combat these prejudices is to recognize our own, and do our best not to let them interfere with our interactions with people.

Often when someone falls into a category of people

that we don't particularly care for, we judge him or her instantly. We will not take the time to get to know that someone as an individual. This is really too bad. This person may have a valuable contribution to make to our lives. A woman named Diane, who moved to America from Russia, told me of how she baked a cake for her new neighbor who had just moved in next door. The woman took the cake, thanked her, and then ignored her when they passed each other on the street the next day. Diane was confused and a little bit hurt, so she asked another neighbor if she knew why this woman behaved this way. The other neighbor hemmed and hawed, and finally said, "Diane, I like you very much and I am glad we're friends, but the new woman just doesn't like foreigners. She feels they take jobs away from hard-working Americans." Diane is one of the kindest, warmest people you could hope to have as a neighbor. She collects people's mail if they go out of town, and even watches the cat for the woman upstairs on occasion. The new woman who moved in will never be able to benefit from the emotional rewards that a friendship with Diane would provide.

Accepting others means giving people the benefit of the doubt, and taking the time to find out the truth. It's better to ask questions than to judge someone quickly only to find out our judgments were way out of line. If the brass paperweight is missing from your desk, don't assume that the cleaning crew took it and look down on them every time you see them. Ask them if they saw your paperweight. If a friend said she'd call you right back, and doesn't, don't assume that she doesn't want to be friends with you. Call to find out; maybe she just forgot.

Instead of asking her boyfriend why he never showed up for their date, Josie simply hung up on Bob when he called the next morning. This went on for three days until he simply stopped calling. He had been in a minor car accident, and didn't regain his composure until the next morning, and then he called her. Instead of asking her employee why he was late three mornings in a row, Margaret simply fired him. The employee's sister had entered an alcohol detoxification center and the employee visited her every morning. He was embarrassed to tell Margaret. Instead of finding out why Jennifer was giving her the cold shoulder, Ellen decided to ignore Jennifer altogether. Jennifer had been told that Ellen was trying to horn in on her business contacts. Jennifer should have confronted Ellen instead of giving her the cold shoulder, but Ellen also should have tried to find out why Jennifer was behaving that way. The cost of judging people too quickly is very high. We have absolutely nothing to lose, and everything to gain, if we take the time to ask questions.

Stop Fixing People

You should see people's flaws as challenges for your own growth. If you are dating someone and he lets you carry the conversation the whole time, instead of trying to fix him by nagging him to talk more, see it as a challenge to draw him out. If you have been dating your girlfriend for two years and you won't marry her because she is overly emotional, instead of making her suppress her feelings, make it a challenge to learn how to listen. If your mother constantly says things that annoy you, instead of pouting, make it your challenge to learn how to communicate your feelings in a relationship. Many people try to fix people because it gives them a feeling of superiority. But trying to fix people is exhausting for you, and annoying to others. When you have the urge to fix someone, say to yourself, "What challenge to my own growth do I see here?"

We need to learn how to love people for who they are. If you find yourself so entrenched in the habit of fixing people that it seems impossible to stop, realize this: Just because someone is in a relationship with you does not give you permission to fix them. If you don't like them the way they are, you can leave. This may sound harsh, but we take far too many liberties with other people's feelings, and we need to learn to respect and appreciate people, flaws and all.

However, there is a difference between "fixing" someone and trying to assist them in growth. Fixing someone makes us feel superior, makes others feel bad, and gives us the opportunity to dominate the relationship. Assisting someone in growth is done gently because we care about another person's welfare. We would never foist our opinions on someone. We might say, "Jesse, I enjoy being with you very much. But sometimes, when you get angry, you become a little hostile. Maybe there is something that I am doing that provokes you. I am mentioning this because I want us to be closer. If you want to talk about it, great. If not, do you feel like watching that movie on television?"

Even though you may have had the habit of "fixing people" for a very long time, try to stop yourself mid-sentence next time. If you are in the middle of telling someone what you think they should do, stop yourself and finish with, "I don't know. Maybe I'm butting into your business." Or if you are yelling at someone because they are late picking you up for the third time in a row, stop yourself and change your tone. "Well, Andrew. I guess my nagging isn't productive. I don't know what to say. All I know is that it hurts my feelings when you come late, as if you don't care enough about me. I know you get tied up with work, but I don't know how not to get upset when you show up late." Chances are that the second method will be much more productive than the first.

Let Go of Expectations

Learn to let go of your expectations by getting rid of unrealistic fantasies. Many people are more committed to their fantasies than they are to finding someone who will truly make them happy. They have certain "pictures" of what their ideal mate will look like and be like, and anyone who differs from that fantasy certainly must not be "the one." The problem is that the person who is "the one" will absolutely never look like or be like what we picture. So therefore we are unable to accept "the one" when they really come along. Accepting others means letting go of our fantasies and trying to learn about another person.

Patricia had dated the captain of the football team in high school, and the president of the student body in college, as well as the top track star. When she was in the business world, she dated very worldly men with fabulous careers. Her ideal husband would be a gorgeous, well-dressed man who drove a very expensive car. He would be so successful in his own business that he could take time off from work any time he felt like it to be with her. And he would dote on her with flowers and chocolates. As Patricia had dated these kinds of men before, she felt she deserved to marry someone with these great qualities. As you already know, these "qualities" have nothing to do with long-term happiness. But worse, Patricia is so attached to her fantasies that she may never be able to find "the one." If you want to be close to another, forget your fantasies, make a top-ten list of your needs, accept someone for who he/she is, and see if that person matches your top-ten list. That is how you will know you have found "the one."

We have all heard of a self-fulfilling prophecy. That is when you believe so strongly that something is going to happen you actually prompt it into happening. For instance, a man who says, "I just know I'm going to fail that test. I don't have what it takes, and it is too difficult," will fail the test. Or a woman wants to go out with a particular man but she thinks, "I know he doesn't like me. Why should he? I am not even going to go over to speak with him, what's the point? He won't ask me out anyway." Of course he doesn't ask her out. Self-fulfilling prophecies are the result of our projecting our own feelings onto reality, and they have the result of making reality look the way we projected.

The same is true with expectations. When we meet someone, we often see what we want to see rather than what is actually there. If a tall and handsome man greets us at the door with a bouquet of roses and many compliments, we see someone who we would love to be in a relationship with rather than taking the time to get to know him. Maybe we should wonder how many women he had to date to perfect his techniques that so impressed us? Instead of trying to impress him for the rest of the evening so that he remains enamored of us, we should spend the evening asking him questions that will reveal his character. Such as, "What are the most important things in your life?" or, "What do you think you will be doing in five years?" or "Have you ever done any type of volunteer work?" Seeing what is truly there, instead of what you wish was there is vital for your happiness. Think about what your expectations are, and be more intent on knowing the truth, because if you let them deceive you, you have no one to look to but yourself. Every doormat has a welcome sign on it.

Expectations are probably at the root of much more misery than anyone suspects. Many of my students shared their ideas of what they are looking for in a mate with me and their expectations are often very unrealistic. They are looking for "Mr. or Ms. Perfect." When someone doesn't match their expectations they move onto someone else rather than taking the time to really get to know the person to see whether that person might be able to make them happy.

When you are thinking, *I gave her a gift for the holidays, she better give me one in return*, stop yourself and think, *I gave her a gift because she has been a good friend to me. It would be nice if she gave me one too, but I am not going to expect it.* Or if you are thinking, *This guy Sheila fixed me up with sounds so handsome. I am going to impress him with my new red dress,"* think instead, "I am looking forward to this date, but I am not going to expect this man to be as handsome as Sheila said, and I am also not going to let myself get all caught up in superficial things. *I am not going to expect anything, I am going to ask questions to see if he matches my top-ten list of needs.* By lessening the power that expectations have over us, we give ourselves the power to not only explore who a person really is, but also to give us the freedom to be ourselves.

There are some people who live very comfortably, but because they expect to be very rich in the future, they cannot enjoy their current lifestyles. Even though they have a new car, it wasn't the fancy one that they expect to own in the future, so they don't get as much pleasure from their new car. Their expectations are keeping them from fully enjoying their lives.

I have had many students tell me that they fell in love with people who had serious character flaws, but that they expected them to change eventually. The relationships never really developed well. There was a constant battle between how things were, and how one partner wanted them to be. It is far better to let go of expectations, and to accept things the way they are. This will make you more content with your life, and give you more peace about what is to come in the future.

NOTEBOOK

- How much do you rely on first impressions?

- How do you think others perceive you the first time they meet you and how accurate is that impression of you?

- What prejudices do you have?

- What do you fantasize about? Do you feel that those fantasies may be keeping you from finding happiness?

- How do your fantasies compare to your top-ten list of needs?

Getting Along With Others

Ken sat down at the kitchen table with his coffee and began to read the newspaper. He could hear Monica sobbing quietly in the living room. He felt a pull to go into the other room but he just sat at the table rereading the same sentence over and over again. Finally, he looked up and saw her standing in the doorway clutching a bunched-up tissue in her fist. "Are you happy now?" she asked. "It's too late to go to the party anyway, and I'm not going looking like this." "We could have gone," Ken answered her, trying to avoid her glare. "Oh, yeah right, and you would have been a barrel of laughs the whole evening." "I said I was sorry," Ken tried. "I just hate these affairs where everybody is trying to outdo each other." "Well it's part of my job, and even before we got married you knew I'd need your support. I guess I'll have to find someone else to go with from now on." Ken's face registered shock for a tenth of a second, and then he turned his head back to his newspaper.

With a sense of satisfaction, Monica walked over to the stove and poured herself some coffee. She busied herself by washing a spoon and getting a napkin from the cabinet. She realized that if she wanted to continue the conversation, she would have to be the first to speak. She leaned against the counter, trying to think of what to say. She looked over at Ken. His shirt collar was twisted and she resisted the urge to go over and straighten it for him. He turned the page of the newspaper as if he was in the middle of a very important article. She stared at him, waiting for him to look up, to help her, but he just sat there engrossed in his paper. After what seemed like an eternity, Monica put her coffee mug down onto the counter. In one fluid movement, she pushed herself away from the counter, up the staircase, and into their bedroom. She closed the door loudly behind her.

Handle Conflicts Together

In handling conflicts together, act like a team, even when you don't feel like it. Ken and Monica seem like they are on opposite sides of a war. They act indifferently, they dramatize their words, they strive to get the upper hand. They posture and jockey for position as if they care more about winning than about each other. But they are under the mistaken notion that the problem belongs to the other person. Even if this issue of not wanting to go to the party is entirely Ken's fault, it is still equally Monica's problem. Placing the blame and making each other the bad guy just causes friction and pushes you apart. Being a team means that any problem either of you has belongs to both equally.

If Ken and Monica had acted like a team, it would look like this: Ken would absolutely never leave a room when Monica is crying. If he had left, not realizing she was upset, he would go back into the living room when he heard her sobbing. When Monica entered the room, he would realize that it must have been difficult for her to swallow her pride and make an attempt to communicate, so he would make it easier for her by saying, "Why don't you get some coffee and sit here next to me." When Monica walked into the room, she shouldn't have spoken harshly by saying, "Are you happy now?" which made it hard for Ken to be supportive. And when he replied, she shouldn't have used sarcasm ("Oh, yeah right . . ."), which puts him further on the defensive.

Additionally, the remark about finding someone else to go with was uncalled for. It made it obvious that she was more interested in hurting him than she was in solving the problem. Maybe she said it to get back at him for leaving her crying in the living room, but as you can see, these posturings are driving them further and further apart. Then, Ken, understandably but wrongly, looks down at his paper and begins to ignore her, which just exacerbates the situation. He should have at least looked up when she was leaning against the counter. This then would have inspired Monica to be kinder to him. Often we are afraid to be too kind for fear that we will be taken advantage of, and in the short run, we might be. But over time, the beneficiary of our kindness will often begin to appreciate us beyond measure, and will reciprocate.

Monica's final departure ends all hope of this issue being solved speedily and with minimum pain. She should have apologized the very moment she made her remark. Indulging ourselves in "temporary insanity" and saying horrible things to someone in anger is extremely damaging. There is never an excuse for a nasty remark and we should strive never to make any. But if they do come out, then the most important thing to do is apologize immediately. Every second we wait to apologize causes more and more damage. But often, we wait to let the pain sink into the other person, or we feel backed into a corner and are forced to defend what we have said. But these remarks always make a situation worse. Ken and Monica had a simple disagreement over what to do about Monica's parties. Now they have to deal with Ken leaving her crying, and Monica making nasty remarks and storming out of the room. Apologizing quickly brings you back together as a team so you can resolve the issue that needs resolving, rather than work on all the subsequent problems that were created.

People tear each other apart when they are on opposite sides of an issue. As a team, they not only come up with better solutions to the problems, but the process of working together strengthens their relationship. When you have a conflict, the last thing you feel like doing is being supportive. But that is when it is most important. It is so easy to indulge our anger at someone else's expense, especially if they deserve it. Ken had made Monica miss the party; the last thing she probably felt like doing was being kind to him. Think how the evening would have turned out if Monica had come into the kitchen and said, "Ken, I know that you don't like to go to parties, and I know I am not very understanding about it, but maybe we can come to a compromise together?" Or if Ken had walked out into the living room and said, "I'm sorry if I hurt your feelings, but this has been bothering me for a long time, and I know it wasn't right to take it out on you. Maybe we should think of a solution like going to every other party or something. I don't know, but let's not have this fight every time we have to go." Acting like a team will make life much more enjoyable because you won't have to go through the rough spots alone.

Handle conflicts together by not withdrawing from one another. Withdrawing is the first thing that we want to do when a conflict arises. But it always makes matters worse. Not only because it hurts the other person, but because getting to where you are discussing an issue is half the battle. Once you walk away, getting there again becomes twice as difficult. We have all been the recipients of a phone being hung up on us, or of someone abruptly leaving the room when they don't like the way the discussion is going. We know how frustrating it is and how much anger it creates. The solution is that we must never be the ones to withdraw, and we must make an agreement with those close to us never to withdraw from a conversation.

There are some people who actually push us to withdraw. They have such a difficult time communicating, and they dislike conflicts so much, that they say anything they can in order to push us away. Sometimes they can even be hostile and verbally abusive. In that case, you can leave if you have to, but before the next conflict arises, sit down and talk to them about their hostility and any solutions the two of you might come up with together. Let them know that every time a conflict arises, they "chase" you out of the room. They may have been blaming you for years that you always bolt.

Whatever the case, you need to set up ground rules for communication. For example, no one is allowed to raise his/her voice, say cruel things, leave the room, or hang up the telephone until the issue is resolved. Whatever rules you create, they must be mutually agreed upon, and you need to support each other in keeping them. If the other person starts yelling, you need to say, "This conversation was actually productive, but when you started yelling I got the urge to leave, and I want to honor our ground rules so let's go back to talking without raising our voices. Did I say something that made you angry which caused you to raise your voice?" Or if you start to leave your partner may say, "Listen, we agreed not to leave the room in the middle of a discussion. I am sorry I started to raise my voice, I guess I am sick of talking about this issue when I can't see a solution. But I will try my best not to yell again. Let's see this problem to the end."

In some relationships, withdrawing is so much a part of how two people interrelate that in a conversation, both parties know it is just a matter of time until one of them walks out. Think for a moment about what kind of effect this has. No one can truly say what he or she is thinking because if one opens up too much, the other will bolt. Or if one begins to talk about issues that are vital to their happiness, he or she can't trust the other person to stick out the conversation. This is devastating to the relationship. Again, ground rules need to be discussed before a conflict arises. In this way a level of trust that neither party thought possible will build in the relationship.

Don't hold grudges. In Ken and Monica's case, it is obvious their conflict did not begin that night. All along Ken has resented having to go to her parties, and Monica has been angry at his lack of support. So instead of sitting down and coming up with a compromise, they hold grudges against each other. A grudge is like a time bomb waiting to go off. That is why it is so important to discuss what is bothering you as soon as you can.

If you are sitting at work and realize that it really bothers you that your best friend always puts you on hold to talk with someone else, make a note to discuss it with her later. If you are in the middle of an argument and someone says, "You always snap at me," which really bothers you, wait until a later time, and then sit them down to talk. Let her know that you have been working hard at not being abrupt and you don't feel that she has even noticed your efforts. Tell her that when she brings it up in an argument you feel that she is using it like a weapon to hurt your feelings.

And it is important that you always bring these issues up before the next time you are in the middle of a conflict. During an argument, it is often difficult to see someone else's side of the story, and your friend will think you are just bringing the issues up now to win the argument. If you do it beforehand, tempers won't be short, the other person will listen, and you can share your feelings without fear of attack. When we hurt each other (which is to be expected in every relationship), we cannot expect that the hurt will go away by itself. We need to heal the pain, and resolve the issues which are causing that pain. If we insist on holding grudges, we damage our relationships.

Make It Safe

Train yourself to read another's mood. Most of the time it is very difficult to think about anything but ourselves. If we are upset about something, or if we are angry, we think the world should stop spinning and everyone should pay attention to us. This is natural. Maybe we should try to be less self-centered, but even if we forget about others and think only about ourselves, we still need to consider when the most likely time is for us to get what we need. If I go barreling into the room, ranting and raving about my needs when my friend just lost her job, am I really likely to get what I need?

When I was first married, an aunt who had been married for thirty-five years told me that I should always wait until after my husband has eaten a full meal before I discussed any important topics with him. At the time, I passed it off as old-fashioned advice, certainly not applicable to men and women of our generation. How wrong I was! It is some of the best advice I ever received. Why? Because people have moods, and moods have effects on how they process information. And if we learn to read others' moods well, not only will we get what we need more often, but we will make our loved ones feel safe around us. They know that we will be sensitive to their moods and that we won't clobber them over the head with information that they aren't in a mood to handle. At a later time, when moods are calmer, that same information will be like water going off a duck's back. And this also works both ways. The more sensitive we are to others' moods, the more sensitive to our moods they will become, and the safety and peace that follows is worth its weight in gold.

Don't put others on the defensive. It's hard to resist the urge to attack people. Our lives are full of hassles. Someone cuts us off on the freeway, a rude stranger knocks our groceries out of our arms and keeps walking, our boss had a fight with his wife so he is grouchy and mean to us. By the time we get home, it is a wonder we don't just let out a scream! (Maybe some of us do.) We must be aware of this frustration because we often let it out on the first person in our way. It is especially convenient if someone does something to annoy us. Then we can overreact and explode, and get rid of our frustration and feel perfectly justified in doing so.

But there is a cost. We can terrify those that we care most about. They can seem able to take our abuse, but inside their self-esteem gets lower and lower, and our relationship is crumbling. They don't trust us to take care of their feelings, and little by little they pull away from us. There is only one solution: Commit yourself to making it safe for others to be around you. If you have had a frustrating day, preempt your attack by walking in the door and saying, "I have had an excruciating day. I am telling you this because the last thing I want to do is take it out on you!" Immediately, they will feel safe and secure, and will be supportive instead of afraid and closed off from you.

Putting someone on the defensive makes it impossible for the issue to be resolved. The person is so busy defending him or herself that they don't have time to even think about a solution to the problem. We have all heard the expression, "It is not what you say, but how you say it." This is probably one of the most significant factors in solving conflicts peacefully. Which would you rather hear: "You always have to be right! No matter what the argument is, the minute you start losing you start insulting me, making me so mad I want to leave the room," or "Maybe we should talk about how we discuss things. I know I have a short temper, and I'll try to curb it more. But when you start insulting me it hurts my feelings. Maybe we should try to figure out a way where I don't lose my temper and we can resolve our problems without getting angry."

Refraining from putting someone on the defensive takes practice. We are so used to stepping into the "attack mode" that it takes some serious effort to focus on the best way to find a solution to a problem. Before we approach someone, we need to think, "What is the best way to get our point across and solve this conflict without putting the other person on the defensive?" Sometimes it means not bringing up the issue when the person is not in the right frame of mind for discussion, sometimes it means taking most of the blame yourself just for the sake of coming to a resolution, and sometimes it means using humor to get your point across.

Instead of saying, "This is the third time in a row you forgot to take out the trash!" say, "Hmm, something smells funny in the kitchen . . ." Instead of saying, "You never wipe your feet at the front door," try saying, "Oh gee, it looks like somehow this mud got all over the carpet, I wonder how that could have happened?" Instead of saying, "You never call me back when I call and I'm sick of it," say, "I guess all that advice that you're giving the president is keeping you so busy on the phone that I totally understand why you don't return my calls." Which would make you feel less defensive? And, as we know, people hate to be told what to do and to have anything demanded of them. Using humor or slowly coaxing them to meet your needs is ten times more pleasant, and ten times more effective.

And don't you be defensive either. As difficult as it is to learn not to put others on the defensive, it is certainly as difficult to learn how not to be defensive yourself. We erroneously believe that if we defend ourselves from attack, the attacker will back down. But the opposite is true. Since we have put up a wall to block out their harsh words, he or she assumes we haven't heard what was said, so it is said louder and harsher than the first time. If instead, we take the attack, nod our heads, and think about what was said, the attacker will immediately back down. It doesn't make it right that we were attacked, but the more we listen, the easier our partner will feel in sharing his or her most intimate thoughts, knowing you are listening, and without fear of your being defensive. This is a very special place to get to in a relationship in terms of closeness and trust.

Let Go of Pettiness

Let go of pettiness and focus on workability. We have all been brought up in a society that focuses on winning. For better or worse, winning has become the all-consuming passion. Become the president of your company, the best skier in your club, owner of the biggest house, the fanciest car, and make the most money. Is it any wonder that we try to win every argument? Instead of focusing on what really matters—the relationship—we focus on using whatever tactics we can to win the battle. In the process, we sacrifice what we all seem to be searching for in the first place—peace and contentment.

Workability means being more committed to the relationship than to being right. It means listening more and accusing less. It means not insisting on having your way, and taking the blame for something even if you don't think it is entirely your fault. It means asking questions instead of accusing, and not getting caught up in petty grievances that aren't really important but that provide you with an opportunity to make the other person wrong. Workability means that you have the power to loosen the grip "winning" has on you for the sake of being closer to people.

Danielle took a class that I gave. She shared with the group that she wanted very much to learn how to get along with others, but her only role models, her parents, fought constantly about everything. She said she couldn't even imagine what it would be like to have a relationship in which two people were more committed to each other than to being "right." Another student, Grace, mentioned to Danielle that she wished her parents had fought constantly, at least they would have been communicating. Grace said that even when one parent was bursting with anger, in her family, it was not okay to let your feelings out. The best role model lies somewhere in between. If we are upset about something, it is important to talk about it. But it is much more productive to talk about it in a nondestructive way. It is also important to realize when we are being petty. Many times we pick a fight over something that we really don't care that much about just so we can be right and "win."

Put things in perspective. It is easy to get enraged over something, thinking that it is vital to your happiness. It is only afterwards that you realize that you have alienated your loved one, pushed her far away from you, and that the issue really wasn't that important to you. It certainly was not worth the result it achieved. Putting things in perspective means making sure that before you go to bat on an issue, you consider whether it is worth your energy. If someone keeps leaving dirty clothes on the floor, don't melo-dramatize the situation by saying, "You must have no self-respect! I cannot live with someone who doesn't respect my space either. I know you do it just to make me miserable and I am not willing to put up with it any longer!" Melodrama and threats waste a lot of energy, especially for such a minor issue. Instead say, "I'll make you a deal. If you keep your dirty clothes off of the floor, I will make the coffee from now on." Done. The times when we can truly get someone to listen to us and have a heart-to-heart discussion with them about our needs are very precious. Putting these issues into perspective will make it clear that using these times for petty concerns is truly wasting them.

Be kind first, think later. I am asked very often, "Should I call him or wait until he calls me?" "She sent me a card, should I send one back?" "He didn't call when he said he would, should I wait or call him?" The answer is, one can never be too kind. There is no need to play games and to second guess what others are thinking. Just be as kind as you can be, and if it is not reciprocated, then stop being kind to them, be kind toward people who will appreciate it and reciprocate. But always be kind first, and think later. Somehow, being kind seems to make us less prone to being petty. Life is so short and I see so many people arguing over insignificant matters. Life would be so much more pleasant if we didn't get annoyed by every little thing, and instead put our energies into being kind and giving.

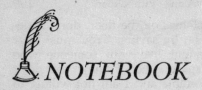

NOTEBOOK

- Do you know how to compromise?

- What grudges have you been holding onto that you'd be willing to let go of now?

- Can you read another's mood?

- Do you put others on the defensive and are you defensive?

- Which petty issues will you push to the side the next time they come up?

Supporting Others

The coach threw her gym bag on the grass without looking down. She was watching Amy round the corner of the track. The girl kept swinging her left shoulder back as she landed on her right leg. It was a habit that was keeping her out of all the finals. As she neared, Coach Lewis lunged her whole body forward and yelled, "Go go go go!" in short loud bursts. Amy smiled as she raced by and headed for the finish line. But her determination wasn't enough to pull her into the lead and she finished third of four racers.

Coach Lewis was waiting for her with a towel and water bottle at the finish line. She tossed them into Amy's hands as Amy went by, walking off her remaining energy. When Amy resumed a normal breathing pattern, she strolled back to the finish line to where Ms. Lewis was standing. "I can't believe you came. You're the best." Amy squeezed more water into her mouth and wiped her forehead with the towel. "Did I pull my arm back?" she asked. "Yup," said the coach. Amy nodded slowly with emphasis as if to say, "I knew that's why I came in third." "Well you made it to States, that's more than most people can say," Coach Lewis said comfortingly. "And I've still got the 500 which is my best race," Amy said. The coach nodded her agreement. The coach grabbed her gym bag and the two women walked up the stairs in cadence and went into the locker rooms.

Just Be There

One of the single, most powerful ways to build a relationship is to just be present. It doesn't matter that Amy came in third place in her race. The relationship she has with Coach Lewis will probably strengthen her for the rest of her life. Showing up means putting aside your obligations, your agenda, your needs, and going out of your way to support someone. It is so easy to get caught up in our lives and to rationalize not supporting another by saying, "It doesn't matter if I go or not, it's going to be a big birthday party and I won't even be missed." And then we wonder why our friend doesn't feel close to us, or why, when it is our birthday, that person doesn't show up to our party.

Sometimes what we are doing seems so much more important than being there for others. A friend asks you to come over to her house on Tuesday night because a man she likes is going to drop by, and she wants your opinion of him. Fine, no problem. But then you hear of an incredible job opportunity and the application has to be delivered by ten the next morning. That means that if you go to your friend's house you'll probably be up all night and you should cancel, right? Wrong. If you cancel, your friend will know that she cannot count on you to be there when she needs you. Showing up shows your friends that they are a priority in your life. Your support gives her the strength to feel self-confident in front of the man who is expected Tuesday night. Think how rattled and insecure she would feel if you canceled out on her and she had to sit waiting by herself. Obviously if someone did that to you, you would be upset and wouldn't feel very good about the relationship. You also wouldn't feel like being supportive in the future.

Carol told me that her best friend moved across the country and got engaged. At the time, Carol was between jobs and was really scraping by. Her friend asked her to come for the wedding and be in the wedding party. Carol could not see how she could possibly afford it. Buying a plane ticket would have been difficult enough, but staying in a hotel and buying the bridesmaid's dress would have been impossible. She simply had to decline. Her friend was very understanding, and offered to loan Carol the money, but Carol's pride got in the way, and she said she couldn't do that to a new bride. Carol told me this story four years after the fact, and she has regretted not going to the wedding ever since. When she thinks back on how important the relationship was in her life, she cannot believe that she let anything stand in her way. She could have taken a bus, she could have arranged to stay with friends, she could have declined to be in the wedding party to save the money on the dress, but at least she would have shown up. The two women are not very close anymore. Carol said that maybe that is the natural course when a friend moves so far away, but had she gone to the wedding, that would have made the biggest statement to her friend that she truly valued the relationship and was willing to do whatever it took to keep it together.

Learn to listen to others. Sam walks into the house and plops himself down on the couch. "I've just been fired," he says. "Well why?" Justine asks incredulously. "I think my boss wants to promote Morgan to my spot." "That's incredible! Morgan's a loser! You've been there for four years, they can't do this to you. And Mr. Josephs knows that we're not going to take this lying down! Our attorney will hear about this! And at that picnic last week, Mrs. Morgan was so sweet to me! Of all the nerve! I'll see to it that she doesn't golf in our group ever again! They don't know who they're dealing with!" Sam shut his eyes and leaned his head into the back of the couch. "Sam, are you listening to me? We'll show them. Mr. Josephs doesn't know it but I met *his* boss, Mr. Croft, at the Shellys' last month. I'll show him who's boss! And that new line you were bringing out, forget it now! That was their new great hope. See if it even makes it out the door without you."

Contrast that scenario with this: Sam walks into the house and plops himself down on the couch. "I've just been fired," he says. "Oh. I'm sorry," Justine says, taking his briefcase out of his hand and putting it next to the table. "What happened?" "I think my boss wants to promote Morgan to my spot." Justine sits down on the couch across from him. "What do you think about that?" she asks. "Well, I'm not sure what to think. About two months ago, Mr. Josephs let me know that they were thinking about getting a fifth vice president at the firm. At the time, I thought he was hinting to me to go to Croft to fight for the spot, but I didn't want to make waves. The spot has not been filled. Maybe Josephs fired me to push me into confronting Croft. I don't know." Sam shut his eyes and leaned his head into the back of the couch. "Well don't worry about it Sam, we'll do fine. You're probably right. Your new product line is too valuable to them to let you go so suddenly. Let's have some dinner, and we'll worry about it later."

Listening means to forego what you want to say in favor of letting another speak. It means asking prompting questions, and then letting others express themselves fully without fear of constant interruption. It means that they can say how they feel without fear of your trying to fix or solve their problems.

Rather, let them come up with their own solutions and maybe just offer suggestions. Let them tell you how they feel about something even if you don't like hearing it. People need to have the freedom to tell you that they don't like the way you treat them, or that they are sick and tired of your temper without causing you to throw a temper tantrum. People need to know they can share things with you that may not make them look good, like, "The reason Mike won't speak to me is because I lied to him about where I was Saturday night and he won't forgive me." If you respond, "You know Mike is right, that was a terrible thing to do," you will push this person away from you. Listening means just letting someone express him/herself fully, without comment or judgment from you.

Sometimes you need to know when to be silent. In a relationship, because we know the other person well, we feel obligated to share all our thoughts and feelings. This is good, as communication is the very fiber that creates a relationship. But there are times when just being there with a person is enough. If someone is terribly upset and crying, just being there will bring comfort. It is not necessary for you to begin a diatribe as to why she shouldn't be crying. Wait until she is ready to talk, or you might even prompt her by saying, "Tell me what's going on?" Or if someone just lost a relative, the most poignant thing you can say is, "I'm sorry." Then just be there with that person. If she wants to talk that's fine, if not, just sit and comfort her. Or if someone has just screamed at you for ten minutes, rather than screaming back, just be silent. Your willpower may inspire him in the future, and it will also give him time to think about his behavior. Many times, your silence will assist others in apologizing. Or if everyone has just seen a very moving play at the theater, walk to your car in silence. Don't feel obligated to blab your opinions all over everybody. Or if you come home from work, having just received a raise, and you find your roommate lying on the couch sleeping with three chocolate bar wrappers crumpled at her side and the want ads circled in red, you might save your news for another time. The point is that being silent and just being there for someone can be a very powerful way to show your support.

Assist Others to Fulfill Their Potential

Take the time to assist others in fulfilling their potential by asking questions. It is very tempting to create an agenda of what we would like to see others accomplish. Instead of responding, "Well, it's a good thing you broke up with him. He wasn't good enough for you anyway," say, "Oh, I'm sorry. How do you feel about that?" Or instead of saying, "I think that job would be too stressful for you," say, "What do you think about that job?" Instead of saying, "You should apologize to him," say, "What do you think can be done to rectify the situation?" Asking questions not only lets another express himself and have his own opinion, but it allows him to create his future, rather than having one imposed on him by you.

Asking questions also gives you a chance to learn of people's needs. Phoebe's boyfriend seemed to be the most wonderful man on earth. He brought her flowers, he took her to concerts and fancy restaurants, and he would surprise her with gifts all the time. When I asked Phoebe whether he met her emotional needs, she didn't understand the question. So I asked her if he was there for her when she was upset about something, or if they had a disagreement, did he call her to make sure she was all right afterward, or, on the other hand, did he put his own needs in front of hers all of the time?

Phoebe didn't know the answers to these questions, but she did say that if an emergency came up at work he would cancel the date at the last minute. She told me this happened all the time. And when I asked if he ever came to see Phoebe at the craft show where she sold her handmade jewelry, "Not yet," was the reply. Her boyfriend seemed like a dream until we realized that he cares for her only in ways that are convenient for him. Maybe it is better to have someone help us take out the trash than bring us flowers.

Assist others in fulfilling their potential by offering help. If someone wants to be a freelance photographer, buy him a book on photography. Go to the store with him and help pick out a camera. Introduce him to anyone you know who might be able to help. Gather information at the library on how to become a freelance photographer, and drive him to his first interview. If your friend says that he wants to learn to be more patient, find the topic for him in a "how to" book. Praise him when you notice that he doesn't honk his horn at a rude driver. If someone you know wants to get married, help her write her personal ad. If she is staying home Saturday night, invite her to a dinner party and seat her next to available men. Be there to listen when she comes home from a horrible date. Raise her spirits when she wants to give up, and introduce her to anybody and everybody you know! If we were all left to fulfill our potentials by ourselves, we would never get there. Helping another fulfill his or her potential is one of the most significant and important things you can do to empower that person.

Do your best to refrain from saying disempowering statements. "Oh, it's already Thursday afternoon, you will never finish that report this week." "Gee you look awful, is something wrong?" "You must be a nervous wreck about having to give that speech this afternoon." "As a fellow computer programmer, don't you just hate it when your mind goes completely blank and you just can't figure out where to go?" "Now is the worst time to find jobs in your field, it's not even worth sending your resume out." "Oh the minute you turn forty you'll put on extra weight. You'll see." What do they think, they're brightening up our day? It is positively shocking to hear comments like these that people say all the time. "Oh well, I'm sure you didn't know that it had such a bad track record. At least your new car looks nice." "Did you notice how much rain came down? Oh, don't worry I'm sure the mud will dry up for your backyard party." "You know, I saw the same dress at a discount store for probably half of what you paid for it." Thank you for sharing.

These disempowering statements actually stop people from fulfilling their potentials. They are the kind of statements that ring in their ears long after they have been said, frustrating, angering, and often stopping others from performing at their best. Furthermore, they are absolutely guaranteed to push people away from you.

Next time stop yourself in mid-sentence, and focus on saying something empowering. "You know, the mail is never going to get there on time, it's useless to try to make the deadline. But, I admire you for giving it your best shot!" "You really shouldn't wear peach, it makes your skin look pale. But, that blue sweater you're wearing is a great choice." "Most people who take that test usually fail the first time around. But they aren't as determined as you are, and they also don't have your brains." Can you see how the person listening would feel deflated with the first comments, and strengthened by the second ones? Which type of person do you think he or she would like to spend more time with? And if someone makes negative comments to you, simply say, "I'd prefer to think positively," "I don't agree with you," or even "I'm so glad you shared that with me ..."

Empowering people can be such a pleasure! It is valuable for the people in our lives, it helps us to be closer to others, *and* it gets our focus off of ourselves! Even in the midst of an argument, we can say things that will make others feel good. "It must have taken a lot of willpower not to raise your voice during this fight. I know I was really pushing you to the limit. Thanks." Or, "Boy it's amazing to me how much stamina you have. You haven't looked up since you walked into work this morning!" "You know the one thing that I really appreciate about you is that when I have a problem, you will listen to me and hash it out no matter how long it takes. I think that is a rare quality." "Wow, you're the fastest cashier I've ever seen!" "Listen, I know the event didn't turn out the way we planned, but you shouldn't feel bad. You gave it your best effort, and I've never seen someone as enthusiastic as you on those phones!"

These empowering statements have the power to lift people into being the best that they can be. Empowering statements are designed to bring someone's special quality out to its full expression. It makes someone feel great, and leaves him or her feeling capable, powerful, and enthusiastic.

Let Others Grow

Let others grow by staying out of their way. It is a very delicate balance between supporting another in attempts to empower them, and staying out of the way to give them room to grow. Our inclination is to hover over them to make sure they make every decision correctly. But often it is the mistakes that teach us the most, and often wrong turns lead to the greatest results. More importantly, a person has to have his or her own sense of control.

So how do you stay out of the way? Well, after you have shown up to their events, listened to their problems, asked them questions to get them focused on their goal, offered help, and said empowering things to them, now you just let things work out on their own. If you offered your suggestions as to how to get a job and they don't follow them, don't nag them about it. The best course of action is to remain quiet. This gives them the opportunity to experiment without judgment, to try different approaches and see what is most effective for them, to do things their own way, and to express themselves fully.

Help only when you are asked. This can be frustrating. You have been there for someone, maybe helped her through difficult times, and now here she is falling into the same trap again. Your job is to get her to the starting gate; only she can run the race. If you just sit tight, and be as supportive as you can, eventually she will come to you for help if she needs it. Then rather than saying to you, "I don't need your help, I'm perfectly capable of handling it myself," she will say, "Hey, things didn't turn out the way I thought, can I come over to talk?" Being able to admit she needs you not only says a lot about your friendship, it says a lot about the value of your support.

When people are growing and learning, the typical pattern is that they take one step forward, three steps back, then maybe two steps forward and one step back. It is certainly not a steady march forward. But as we want instant gratification, this can be frustrating and annoying. Rather than be upset or put them down for their mistakes, we should come to expect these difficulties and setbacks, and be supportive through these times in order to help others see that setbacks are a natural part of growth.

When they don't get the job, tell them at least they tried their best. When they finally land another job, tell them you think it is an even better opportunity. When their boss turns out to be mean, tell them to think of it as a challenge, and help them to think of ways to communicate with their boss that might make things better. When they complete a project, acknowledge their fortitude. And even if you gave them step-by-step instructions on how to accomplish something, and they accomplish it, do not take one ounce of credit. They did the hard part, and your taking credit only diminishes them. If they acknowledge you, good for them, but don't expect it. Supporting others is very challenging, and sometimes frustrating, but it is always extremely rewarding. And there is no better spouse than one who supports and empowers his or her mate with kind words and warm gestures.

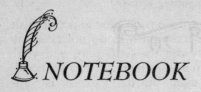

NOTEBOOK

- Are you supportive of your friends and loved ones? Do you listen to them and are you there when they need you?

- Do you assist others in fulfilling their potentials?

- Do you offer help when someone needs it?

Letting Others
Support You

Victoria made coffee every morning for the men in her office; she wasn't about to make some poor secretary spend half the morning in the kitchen. She straightened out her red suit, poured herself a cup of coffee, and went back into her office suite. She could see dozens of high-rises out her windows. Her phone buzzed and her secretary's voice came out of the speaker, "It's Barry." She picked up the line, "Hi, what's up?" "They said your car won't be ready for three days at least. Don't worry, I'll take you to work." "Forget it. What'd they say it'll cost?" she asked. "What do you mean forget it, I said I'd take you to work, how else are you going to get there?" "Barry, I'm not talking about this now. I'll rent a car. What did they say it would cost?" "About eight-fifty," he replied somberly. "Terrific. Anything else?" she asked. "No. I love you." "I love you too," she whispered. "See you later." "Vicky, let me take you," he tried. "Good-bye Barry." "Bye Vic."

Get Off "Independence Mode"

Examine your resistance to support. Many of my female students were brought up during a time when it was politically incorrect to depend on a man. It was the dawn of a new age. Women were breaking into new territories in the workplace, in politics, at home. It was a war of independence and we won. Women have more choices now than in any other time in history. But as in any war, there are casualties. And the casualties of this war are the women who cling so strenuously to their hard-won independence that they cannot allow themselves to enjoy one of the most valuable gifts on earth: letting another support you.

Letting others support us is vital to our well-being. It not only gives us the strength to reach our full potential, but it is vital for a strong, healthy relationship. Supporting another is great, and brings you closer together, but letting him support you makes him feel closer and more attached to you as well. Denying this privilege not only makes the relationship very unstable and unbalanced, but it is also cruel. It is like bringing someone into your home, sitting them at your dining table to a grand feast, and not letting them eat. For a relationship to be fully actualized, both parties must fully support each other.

I am not suggesting that women depend fully on men. The operative word is *interdependence*. You both support each other, you both let the other be supportive, and you end up both needing each other. Needing someone, especially a man, has been verboten for a long time now. It's about time we woke up and realized it's okay. Our lives are much more enriched by needing someone and having that need filled. But what is different from before is that now we both need each other equally.

Examine your own reasons for being resistant to support. Are you caught up in the momentum of not wanting to depend on someone at the expense of your own happiness? Did you depend on someone who left you, that now you won't allow yourself to depend on anyone? Do you and your friends deride women who depend on men?

Victoria, the executive in the red suit mentioned earlier, was a student in a month-long course that I gave. She shared her life with us, and many of the students had similar stories. Victoria's parents divorced when she was eleven. Her mother had never worked a day in her life and the divorce threw the family into a major turmoil. Her mother was depressed and lonely, and so helpless that Victoria vowed to never get into a situation where she depended on a man. She went to college, majored in business, and then went on for her MBA. Now she is the vice president of a publicly-held company. But Victoria is not happy. She can't even let a secretary bring her coffee. Her boyfriend has tried for two years to break down her barrier that keeps him from getting close. Her standard line is, "Just leave me alone. I can take care of myself."

You can get off the "independence mode" by imagining what support would be like. Once Victoria recognizes the reasons for her resistance to support, she can imagine what support would be like. What would it feel like to be driven to work every morning by Barry? What would it be like to have a friend run an errand for her? And what would it feel like to have a secretary bring her coffee, and for her to tell the secretary how much she appreciates her effort and kindness? Being supported really isn't that bad. Does it mean that you owe the person your gratitude? Yes. Does it mean that you should be supportive of them as well? Yes. Is it worth it? Absolutely. You will begin to feel closer to people than you might ever have felt before.

It may take time before you can let yourself be supported, but it is vital to your happiness. Letting others support you is the most empowering thing we can do for them. If they know that they can help you and be there for you, it will absolutely bring out the best in them.

The habit of being independent is so ingrained in our psyches that we constantly have to remind ourselves about the value of being supported. At first, when we begin to let others support us, we will feel hemmed in, hovered over, and almost claustrophobic. We will feel it is more trouble than it is worth because for every act of support we accept, we will feel obligated to give something back. First of all, the claustrophobic feeling is only our discomfort with being supported. Once we get used to it, the feeling will lessen more and more over time, which is a healthy sign. Second, you do not need to keep an accurate accounting of every incident of support. Do not worry about it. It will all work out perfectly if you just support another whenever you can, and let them support you as much as they can. If there is an imbalance, you both will be able to feel it.

It is also valuable to recognize that probably the greatest people of our time, the ones that made the most significant impact in terms of making the world a better place, all had extensive support networks. They did not accomplish such grand dreams by themselves. It would have been impossible for them to have done it alone. Once you are open to letting others support you, you will see that a whole new world of opportunity awaits you. Victoria might have become vice president on her talent and skill, but to truly make a powerful leap, she needs to enlist the support of others.

Think of what Victoria might accomplish. If she let support in, she could have more time to donate to charity, she could become the president of the chamber of commerce where she has sat on the board for four years, she could mentor junior staffers in her office to assist them in their careers, she could visit Terry's mother, who is in the hospital. Getting support puts you in a much more powerful position to make a contribution to others, and to let others feel the power of supporting you. It's time to turn the tide and start to see getting support as a strength, one that has the power to let us achieve our best, and one that has the ability to bring others closer to us in a bond that makes our relationships vital and strong.

Engage Others in Your Life

Engage others in your life by sharing your difficulties. That does not mean to complain wherever you go! It means that in order to enlist others' support, it is helpful that they know what is going on. If you had a big fight with your sister before you arrived to work, instead of snapping at your assistant, you might say, "Listen, if I seem brisk this morning, don't take it personally. I had a terrible morning and I'm a little exhausted." If you are at the market, and you spend more money than you planned, don't take it out on the checkout person. You might say, "Boy, I only came in here for a few things. Wait until I try balancing my checkbook after this!" Others will commiserate with you, and instead of being angry and upset, maybe you will put a smile back on your face. If a car splashes mud on your coat, then a bus almost hits you, and you walk up to your apartment disgruntled, tell your roommate what happened rather than feeling like the world is punishing you for something. Maybe she will make you a cup of hot chocolate.

The point is that we sometimes feel that we carry the weight of the world on our shoulders. Engaging others in our lives makes the difficulties less derailing. They become opportunities to share and commiserate with others, which brings us closer. It's important to realize that when we share difficulties of a more significant nature, it takes a certain amount of trust in the other person. For instance, if we feel that it is unjust that one of our colleagues has received a promotion, sharing this information with the wrong person might be detrimental to our advancement. We need to find a confidant who is removed from the situation and with whom we can share our feelings openly. This helps us get over our resentment, and gives us the strength to publicly congratulate the colleague. If we break up with our boyfriend, we need to find a confidant who will understand us. You might say to your secretary, "Yes, Bill and I broke up, but I think it is probably for the best." And then later, to your best friend, "I can't believe he left me. Just last week he told me how much he loved me. I am so broken up about this I don't know what to do!" Use discretion in your choice of a confidant, but don't be reluctant to share your more trite difficulties with everyone.

There is one area that I would like to caution you about because I have seen this phenomenon happen to many of my students. Be careful of sharing difficulties in your relationships with people who don't want you to have a successful relationship. If we are very close friends with someone, and then we meet a person who is a possible marriage partner, guess who all of a sudden becomes a fifth wheel? Our friend will naturally dislike this person. She has a vested interest in your staying single so that she doesn't feel like she is the only one left who isn't married. We wonder why she picks apart every person you go out with.

Further, if you are using this person as your close confidant in handling issues regarding the relationship, you are just adding fuel to the fire. If the possible marriage partner picks you up late, she will say that the person is irresponsible. If that person does anything mean to you, she will suggest you drop him. Even if that person gives you a gift, she will find a way to fault it. So you need to prioritize what is most important to you: this friend, or having a successful relationship. Sharing difficulties is valuable in letting others support you, just be sure you choose the right people in whom to confide.

Engage others in your life by sharing your successes. Sharing successes with people can be inspiring to them and can bring them joy. If you get a raise at work, share it with your family. If you just threw a charity dinner and it was a sell-out crowd, tell your co-workers. It might inspire them to get involved in activities outside of the office. If you ran your first marathon, tell the woman at the store where you are buying a drink to cool yourself down. It will put a big smile on her face.

For people who have spent their lives trying to project the image, "I've got it all together," sharing difficulties about their lives can certainly pose a problem. But looking closely at why a person would want to project this particular image, it would seem that only a person who *didn't* have it all together would be so intent on projecting that image. You have made such great strides in this book in terms of "getting it all together," so stop worrying about having to project that image. The most significant contribution you can make to others is to just be yourself.

Ask for Support

Ask for support by thinking first about what you need. Often our lives become so overwhelming that we don't even have time to sort out what is bothering us and what we could do to solve it. If you have gained a little weight so that nothing fits quite right, your boss is angry at you for not getting a report finished on time, and you are having a feud with your brother because you insulted his girlfriend, the last thing you want to do is to sit down to think. More likely you want to get absorbed in a television show that will take your mind off of everything. But unfortunately, misery can't be squelched by ignoring it. Even if you only spent five minutes thinking about these issues, or chatted to someone on the phone about them, that would help you not to feel so victimized by the situation. Rather than feeling helpless, you would begin to look for solutions to your situation.

If you need more clothes that fit better, maybe you could ask for a shopping spree from your parents. If you need to join the gym, why not ask a friend to join with you. If you need to set deadlines farther into the future with your boss, why not ask for a meeting to set out a three-month schedule. If you need to make amends with a relative, why not apologize and ask for forgiveness. Think about the solution to your problems, and the closer you are to getting on the other side of them, the more able you are to ask for support.

In terms of having your needs met, it is important to isolate your needs. Each need that you have matches up with its respective fulfillment. There is no such thing as anyone or anything that can fulfill all of your needs in their entirety. Many of my students have a secret fantasy that someone is going to come along and fulfill every single need that they have. They want someone to say, "Everything is going to be fine. You don't have to worry about anything ever again. I will take care of you and all of your problems and needs." They are waiting for someone to come along and relieve them of the anxieties of life. Realistically, no one can do that for us. Don't discount the importance of someone in your life because he doesn't meet all of your needs.

Ask for support by making clear requests. Rather than complaining about something, and hoping someone will come to your rescue, share with them what is going on, and then ask, "Would you mind picking up my dry cleaning from the shop?" Don't say, "I washed all of the dishes last night, I took out the trash this morning, and I picked up groceries on the way home. And what have you done?" Instead say, "Do you mind cleaning the kitchen? I did the dishes, trash and shopping." Don't say, "Last time your car broke down, it took me three hours to get back to work and I got in trouble." Just say, "Do you mind meeting me at my car right now, it broke down." Instead of saying, "Whenever I have a big project at work, you are never there for me. You act as if I'm not stressed out and that you can make all of your usual demands of me. I'm sick of it," say, "I have a big project at work. Do you mind picking up Chinese food for dinner? And, I'm in kind of a bad mood tonight, so please don't demand too much of me, I might snap at you!" And don't be too demanding. That would be issuing orders, not letting others support you. By making your request clear and specific, without putting others down or making them feel bad, you assist them in supporting you to the best of their ability.

Acknowledge others for their support. Sometimes it is difficult for us to acknowledge how much someone has helped us. Maybe we feel thanking someone for his advice diminishes our accomplishment. Maybe we don't want to feel indebted, or feel as if we have to return the favor. Whatever our reasoning, it's always better to show too much appreciation than not enough. Many times when we do something for someone else, we feel like they weren't appreciative enough. It makes us feel distant from them and certainly doesn't make us disposed to being supportive of them in the future. The world is simply too crowded with ungrateful takers for us to join their ranks. We need to stop worrying about managing our acknowledgments and thank anyone who ever helps us for anything.

In this section you have learned how to empower others. It is a time-consuming endeavor. It takes thought and care, and often feels like we are putting out a great deal of energy and getting nothing in return, even though we know, and can instinctively feel, that it is making us a better person, a more valuable member of society, and also a great catch. It takes fortitude and determination to continually empower others. Having accepted ourselves and others, having learned how to get along with others, and having learned how to support and be supported will serve as a powerful foundation from which to build a lifetime of contributing to others and fulfilling our own potential.

NOTEBOOK

- Do you allow others to support you?

- Do you share your difficulties and your successes?

- Do you care what others think?

- Do you ask others for support and do you, in turn, support them?

APPENDIX:
ETIQUETTE PRIMER

After examining the profound subjects of emotional and environmental stability, as well as learning about character traits and empowering others, the study of etiquette seems enormously trite in comparison. Yet if you succeed in improving your character traits only to be rude to the person who dialed the wrong number, what have you really gained? The purpose of this section is to provide you with the fundamental rules of being polite. This will make you more attractive to others and will help you to feel comfortable and confident in any situation.

The great part about this section is that it will increase the speed at which you are able to integrate the other parts of this book into your life. Being polite and acting kindly toward others will give you a sense of pride and confidence that will empower you to work harder on the more meaningful areas already covered. But far more important than following the rules of etiquette is that you do your best to make other people feel comfortable. I know a woman from

New York whose manners are perfect, but she puts on such airs that she makes everyone feel ill at ease. She uses the rules of etiquette to feel superior to others, which pushes them away from her. You want to use these rules to draw people closer to you. This is not only valuable for being a great catch, but it will also make your life more enjoyable.

The rules in this etiquette primer are general guidelines. There are no rules that cannot be broken. If you remember that your primary goal is to make others comfortable, it will be easier for you to implement these guidelines with moderation and flexibility. If everyone at the table is eating fried chicken with their fingers, break the etiquette rules and eat with your fingers. If everyone starts eating from the wrong bread plate, just follow suit. If you feel like a hypocrite for admiring someone's home when you don't care for it, then don't say anything. The most important point is to use thoughtfulness and common sense as your primary guide.

Interaction Satisfaction

How many times have you stood patiently, holding the door for someone walking behind you, only to have them pass you by without a word? Don't you feel like yelling, "You're welcome!" How many times have you told a phone-caller, "Oh, I can't talk right now, can I call you back?" only to have them continue to ramble on as if you've said nothing? And how many times have you been standing in a checkout line holding one red apple, only to have the person in front of you with a basketful of groceries completely ignore you? Everyone is in their own little world, and rather than adding to the problem, maybe we should try to be part of the solution.

When someone goes out of their way for you, always say thank you, whether it is letting you step in front of them at the theater to let you meet up with your friends, or holding the door open for you, or assisting you in picking up your fallen papers. Rather than taking these petty courtesies for granted, recognize that the person did not *have* to do what he or she did. Whenever you make a phone call, always ask the recipient if you have reached them at a good time to talk, and if they say no, say good-bye. It is extremely important to respect others' time.

If you are in an urgent rush, and need to cut ahead of someone in line, apologize and ask permission to cut in. And if someone behind you has a small order, why not make their day? Of course you don't have to let five people through, but letting one or two people through will not only make them happy, but maybe it will inspire them to be kinder to others. It will also give you a feeling of elation, something we all could use more of!

Be as considerate to waiters, cashiers, and other service people as you can. They've been on their feet all day. Try to be courteous to everyone whether you will benefit from it or not. Also, being kind to service people will get you in the habit of being kind in general.

When you are phoning someone, and someone else answers the phone, be sure to say hello to him before you speak to the person you phoned for. To do otherwise is rude. If you phone the wrong number, do not slam the phone down; apologize for the disruption and wait for the other person to hang up first. If someone phones you, and it is a wrong number, simply apologize and tell him he has the wrong number. If he seems confused, spend a moment with him to confirm the number he has dialed. Developing the habit of going out of your way for others will make you a great catch.

If you are inviting your friend to an event, don't ask, "What are you doing Saturday night?" leaving him or her no opportunity to get out of the invitation. First state the particulars of the event, including the location, time, and who else is likely to be there, and then say, "Do you think you might be able to make it?" Also, always try to remember to phone people who are not well. Make a list of such people and post it where you will see it regularly so that when you do have a moment, you can lift someone's spirits. We all know how much it means to us when others think of us and our welfare. By reaching out to others, you will not only be doing a kind act for them, but you will create a closeness so that when you need support, they will be there for you.

Never make the mistake of forgetting to acknowledge a gift that has been given to you. If you can't take the time to write a thank you note or at least call the gift giver, you have no right to take the time to use the item! To accept a gift without thanking the person in writing or by telephone is inexcusable and the mark of a self-centered person. Be sure you respond immediately.

If someone is not courteous to you, do not glare at them. It certainly won't change their behavior. Do your best to overlook others' blunders. Remember, character traits are what is most important; etiquette just assists one to grow one's character traits more easily. To point out another's mistakes is unkind. Teaching others manners when they haven't asked is a sure way to alienate friends. The best that we can hope for is to inspire others by our example.

It is also vital never to embarrass another person under any circumstances. Even if you are trying to embarrass them to teach them a lesson, the ends never justify the means. This act of cruelty will cause endless heartache for both of you. And if you will notice, people who make a habit of embarrassing others are miserable, unhappy people.

Behavior Mortification

Don't *ever* swear, don't chew gum in public, don't wear garish makeup, dress modestly, don't point your finger at people, and don't litter. Never put your handbag on the floor, never scratch your head, rub your face, or clean your fingernails in public. Never drop in on people unannounced. Even if you have driven one hundred miles and happen to be in the neighborhood, call from a phone booth around the corner to see whether your timing is convenient. Never drink and get out of control, never gossip or whisper about others, and never be nosy about other people's business. If you must borrow something, return it quickly and in good condition. Never go to another's house when you have a cold, spreading your germs to everyone. Don't block the road with your car, don't block someone else's car when they need to get out of their driveway, don't honk at people incessantly, and always dim your highbeams for oncoming cars. And if you are picking up a friend to go out, park your car and ring their doorbell rather than honking the horn. Treating others with respect and dignity will endear you to them.

When you are getting into a car, turn your back to the inside of the car and sit into the car first, then swing your legs in after you. If you need to pick something up from the ground, never bend over from the waist, rather crouch down, bending your legs, and retrieve the item. Don't lean against a wall or furniture; stand tall and proud or sit down.

Always do your best to hold your arms in by your side, and never throw your arms over the back of a couch. Try this once, and you will see how much more elegant you feel with your arms in. Never sit on the arm of a couch, and when crossing your legs, try to keep the sole of your shoe facing the ground so someone else doesn't have to look at it.

Never be self-conscious of your body. Of course groom yourself well, but if others judge you on your body or your clothes, they are not people of high quality so don't worry about them anyway. When you walk across a room, do so proudly. If you are going up stairs, a man follows the woman up, and a woman follows a man down, thus if she falls, he can catch her. If a revolving door is moving, the woman gets in first, if not, the man gets in and pushes it for her. The women's movement gave women choices, but it did not make them stronger than men. Stop fighting and do what makes sense.

Also, if someone compliments you, just say, "Thank you," or "That is kind of you to mention it." Don't say, "Oh, this worn-out old dress?" which makes the compliment giver feel as if he must have poor taste. And if you give a compliment, do so thoughtfully. If you say, "Boy, I've never seen you look so good," that implies that they usually look pretty bad. Instead say, "Boy, you look great!" I hear this lament from my students all of the time. "I am such a great catch, why doesn't anyone appreciate me?" The secret is to start appreciating *them*. Go out of your way to compliment others and to show them how wonderful *they* are.

Exhibitionism seems to be very popular, but it is always practiced by people with low self-esteem who need to prove their importance. They speak at the top of their lungs and laugh uproariously with forced laughter. Their movements are sudden and harsh and they make their presence known in a most unpleasant manner. They spend all of their energy to make an impression. Speaking softly and gently is the mark of one who is considerate of others, and doesn't feel the need to broadcast themselves to prove their inner worth. Speaking loudly is bad form in any circumstance except in a medical or other emergency. Further, excessive public display of physical intimacy is in very poor taste, and is a symptom of a very weak relationship if it must be validated in this way.

Hostess Twinkles

Whenever any person sets foot in your home, besides greeting them warmly and taking their coat, the very first question to ask them is what they would like to drink. Proceed to offer them several choices, nonalcoholic, unless you are intending to have some liquor as well. Keep your eyes on their drinks to fill them if they become two-thirds empty. And always try to serve something to eat. Whether it's nuts, candies, or fresh carrot sticks is not important, but your thoughtfulness is. If you are hosting an event, the details of the event, the food, the drinks, the location, are much less important than your warmth and kindness to everyone. Greet all of your visitors and do your best to introduce people to at least a few others so that they may have someone to talk to.

If people show up late, (you only have to hold dinner for fifteen minutes) and if they miss the main course, you may bring them a plate of food while the others are eating dessert. Never serve yourself first, and always eat slowly, waiting for your slowest guest to finish. If only one person takes a second helping, take one as well so that they won't feel responsible for slowing everyone down. If someone spills or breaks something, be as kind as possible. Doing otherwise is fruitless as you cannot undo what has been done, and it will only succeed in making them feel terrible. Just continue speaking as if nothing has happened, as if the conversation is much more important to you than the mess, and as unobtrusively as possible, get whatever supplies you need to clean up. Jumping up and running into the other room will attract everyone's attention and will embarrass your guest. Your kindness will be an inspiration to those around you.

No matter how long a person visits, always walk

your guests all the way out—to their car, the front foyer of your apartment building, the elevator, or maybe down to the lobby. If you have a large party, seeing them to your door and waiting for them to walk a bit away is fine. And don't close the door the minute someone turns his back. You can imagine how good you would feel if someone took the time to do this for you. It makes your guests feel completely taken care of and like you are truly glad that they came.

As a host or hostess, you need to keep the conversation moving along, which is a good skill whether you are hosting or not. One key secret to getting close to people is to lavish them with attention and to make them feel important. The best conversationalists don't start a conversation by saying, "I think ..." but rather, "What do you think of ..." Drawing the other person out is a challenge, but that is the purpose of social interaction. Don't sit at a table telling someone your whole life story. Instead, ask the other people about *their* life stories! Or if you are stuck for something to say, ask another her opinion or advice about something. "What do you think of traveling to Florida in the fall?" Or, "Do you know of a good place to purchase coffee beans?" Or, "I understand you are an engineer. What do you think of that new project downtown?" Whatever the topic, people love to share their thoughts and will consider you a wonderful conversationalist!

You Guest It

The most important thing to remember about being a guest in someone else's home is respect. That means that if they have cared enough to invite you into their home, you should care enough to respond regarding whether you will attend or not. Make yourself a hard and fast rule that you will respond to all invitations on the same day that you receive them. Then you don't have to worry about forgetting to respond. If you are waiting to see if your schedule will permit you to attend, phone the host or hostess to let them know you will let them know in one week or whenever you are due to find out what your schedule is. We all know the agony of trying to plan an event while having no idea how many people will attend. Your host has enough worries without you being one of them.

Never arrive early to an event or it will embarrass your host. The best time is within ten minutes of the scheduled time. And do your best not to be late. If you will be late or must cancel at the last minute, make sure that you call. (This is true for restaurants as well.) Never surprise your host by bringing someone that he or she is not expecting, it could prove disastrous.

If you are going to someone's home or visiting someone in the hospital, you will always feel better if you have a small gift to bring them. Whether it is a small box of chocolates, flowers, wine, a cake, notecards, a cutting board, it doesn't really matter. This is not an obligation, but a host will truly appreciate it and be grateful that someone appreciates the hard work that they have put in to entertain and a sick friend will appreciate your thoughtfulness. If someone throws a special party for you, it is nice to send flowers beforehand, or bring a special gift for them when you arrive.

It is always a good idea to admire someone's home whether you do or not! Even saying, "What interesting things you have!" is better than silence. Don't ever take your shoes off unless it is requested that you do so, and be sure that you never put your feet up onto the furniture. If someone is standing by themselves at a party, introduce yourself to them whether you are interested in speaking to them or not. It is far more important that you be kind than that you scope out the most interesting people to mingle with. And because of how kind you are, you will attract quality people to you at another time that will be much more meaningful than chit-chat at a party.

When you are seated, wait until all have been served their meal before you begin to eat. Watch the hostess. When she begins, you begin. At a large dinner, the hostess ought to say, "Please begin, your food will become cold," but if she doesn't, it is perfectly polite to start after three or four people have been served. If you do not like the food, politely push it around your plate so that it looks like you have eaten. And if you accidentally break something, be sure to apologize and make arrangements to replace the item or pay for the damage.

Never overstay your welcome. If you are with a friend, try to discuss beforehand how long you would like to stay at the event. That eases tensions if you differ on when you would like to leave. If it turns out that he or she wants to leave and you don't, leave together first and argue later. At large parties, always greet the host or hostess and the guest of honor when you arrive, and always be sure to say good-bye to them when you leave, even if you have to search everywhere to find them. This is especially important at weddings and other formal occasions. The hosts are probably so busy that this might be the only time they speak with you personally, and it will make them feel relieved to know that they have done so.

Always phone your hosts to thank them within two days after an event. A notecard is fine, but either way, this common courtesy has fallen out of fashion, and it is really a shame. We all know the anticlimactic feeling of having planned an event for weeks or months only to have it over within a few hours. Knowing that you enjoyed the event will mean more to your host than you can imagine. This level of thoughtfulness on your part will be a bond that brings you together.

Elbows off the Table

Never have your elbows on the table while you are eating. And always hold your arms in, as if you were holding a piece of paper against your sides. Never let your elbows raise up even if you are cutting a tough piece of meat or drinking from a glass. Most people believe incorrectly that the left hand belongs in the lap when it is not in use. The proper position for the left hand is to the left side of your plate, either open or fisted, but never curled up and around the plate. Both hands belong on the table at all times until after dessert when you might push your chair back and fold your hands in your lap.

Your handbag or coat belongs on the back of your chair, on another seat, or on your lap, but never on the table or the floor. Try to sit up as nicely as possible, try not to cross your legs under the table as you might kick someone or put your shoe on the furniture, and never tip your chair onto its rear legs. Women should try not to wear a lot of lipstick to the table as it will stain your napkin and look very unsightly on your glass and flatware. If you carry tissues with you, you can wipe your lipstick off before dinner is served. When you are finished eating, it is perfectly acceptable to put on a little lipstick or powder, but do this as quickly and unobtrusively as possible.

Always chew silently with your mouth closed. Having a closed mouth will make it impossible for you to talk with your mouth full! Never take large mouthfuls of anything. Don't ever put one mouthful of food in on top of another, nor take a drink of anything when your mouth has food in it. The only exception to this is if the food is hot and the liquid will save you from burning your mouth. Also, do your best not to ask questions of another when his mouth is full. And don't cut up your whole meal at one time, it looks unattractive and will make it seem as if you are in a rush.

Bread may be handled with your fingers, but do not spread butter over the entire bread. Break off little bite-sized pieces and butter each piece as you eat it. Taking two bites from one buttered piece is fine. With hot biscuits or toast, it is fine to butter them fully as they will lose the heat necessary to melt the butter. But still take small pieces to place into your mouth. Bread can be quite messy, so take care to handle it carefully so as not to create the need for a new tablecloth! Also, restaurants should really be taken to task for serving us practically an entire head of lettuce with only a chef's feeble attempt to shred it for us. The proper way to serve salad is in nice delicate pieces. But it is perfectly acceptable to cut your salad into smaller pieces, provided you don't end up flinging salad all over the other dinner guests.

Never push back your plate when you are finished eating your meal, and don't assist the waiter in clearing the table by stacking the dishes unless it is impossible for him to reach them. If you have a complaint for a restauranteur, take her aside to let her know. If you have a compliment, feel free to praise her openly. Never stand while you are eating, even if you are in a rush. Some people eat standing if they are alone. But you must make yourself realize that you are a dignified, respectable person, and you should treat yourself as such, even if it means cleaning more dishes and placemats. There is no one that you should treat with more respect than yourself. And it is vital to understand that it is absolutely impossible to have two sets of manners, one for guests and one for our private lives. First, it is excruciatingly difficult to switch sets of manners back and forth. Second, the practice you get at home helps to create good habits. Third, if you have two sets of manners, you will begin to feel like a hypocrite.

Implementing Implements

The moment you sit down at the table, place your napkin on your lap. Women fold their napkins in half diagonally and place the long side parallel to their waists. Men fold their napkins squarely, not in half, but folding them a third down and again placing them parallel to their waists. Never tuck a napkin into your clothing or belt. Use your napkin by gently patting your lips rather than a big wipe across your face. Never use your napkin to blow your nose and only use it to catch a sneeze in an emergency. Keep a handkerchief in your purse or back pocket for these instances. Always blot your lips with a napkin before and after taking a sip of liquid. This may seem excessive, but once this becomes a habit, you will wonder how you ever did it any differently. Keep the napkin on your lap for the entirety of the dinner. When dinner is finished, or if you must leave the table for a moment, place your napkin to the left of your plate. If your plate has been removed after the meal, then place your napkin in the center where the plate had been. Do not refold it, or roll it into a ball, but drape it gently and the folds will help it to sit still. Only place your napkin on the table after a meal, or once your host or hostess has done so to signify the end of the meal.

Always begin your meal by using the implement farthest from your plate. If there are three forks and two knives, the farthest left fork and the farthest right knife would be the proper implements for the first course. Your bread plate will always be to your left, and your glasses will be to your right. During the meal, the proper place to lay your fork is like a clock hand facing three or four o'clock. The proper place for your knife is on the top right third of the plate's

rim. When cutting meat, the fork should be in the
left hand, prongs down, while you cut with your
right hand. You may leave the fork in your left hand,
to eat your meal. Many people find this European
style of eating more convenient than the American
way of switching back and forth.

Never push food onto your fork with your fingers.
It is perfectly correct to use your knife as a pusher
for this purpose. Don't take half a bite from your fork
or spoon, leaving the remainder on the implement for
everyone to gawk at. Take a smaller spoonful instead, especially if it is ice cream and the cold might
tempt you to leave half of your spoonful uneaten.
And don't ever leave your spoon in your cup. Never
use a spoon to eat if a fork will serve the purpose,
or follow the hostess's lead. And don't use your dirty
knife to get butter or jam from a dish on the table,
or use your wet spoon in the sugar bowl for use in
your coffee. Find a clean implement to accomplish
these tasks.

When eating soup, it is fine to tilt your bowl to
get the remainder of the soup, but always tilt it away
from you, and spoon out the liquid away from you
as well. The proper way to hold a wine glass is with
your index and second fingers carrying the weight
of the glass with your third and fourth fingers resting
on the first two fingers all in a neat line. Use three
fingers for larger glasses, and never point your pinky
out. When you are finished with your meal, bring
your knife and fork together, pointing them like clock
hands at five o'clock. Adjust these rules for comfort
if you are left-handed.

Food is always served to a person's left, and plates
are always removed from the right. The exception to
this is glasses, which are served to a person's right
and removed from the right. Trays of food are always
passed the same way, from a person's left to a person's right, or if it is easier to remember, counter-
clockwise. When passing a pitcher, place it in front

of the other person with the handle facing them. And every morsel of food that enters your mouth must come from your own plate. Even if a tray of cookies is passed around, first put the cookie on your plate, or on a napkin, and then raise it to your mouth. If someone at the other end of the table requests a platter, it is impolite to help yourself to that dish first. You may say, "Here it is, and please pass it back to me when you are through." If they say, "Oh, go ahead, help yourself first," then go ahead and do so.

If you come across food that is inedible, the basic rule is that however that food went in is how it should come out. If you ate an olive with your fingers, the pit comes out by your fingers. If you ate a tough piece of meat with your fork, it comes out by your fork. Fish bones and anything difficult to remove by another implement may be removed with the fingers. These items may be placed on the rim of your plate at eleven o'clock. If you have something caught in your teeth, do not use a toothpick or your finger at the table. Wait until after the meal, or if it is unbearable, excuse yourself to the restroom. Finally, when the meal is completed, be sure to thank your host or hostess.

These guidelines are designed to get you started on the road to having the wonderful manners that are appropriate to match the fabulous character traits that you have been developing since the start of this book!

EPILOGUE

You have come a long way since the beginning of this book. You have learned how to get beyond your history and start with a clean slate, how to develop emotional and environmental stability, how to reinterpret your past so as to empower your future. You have learned about strengthening your communication skills, and how to grow into the kind of person you have always wanted to be. You have learned how to express yourself to potential mates honestly and warmly. You have learned how to have great character traits, how to empower others, and how to present yourself in the best light. Most importantly, you have acquired the tools to help you change, grow, and create your own future—tools that you can use for the rest of your life.

At first the amount of work associated with this process may seem overwhelming. But soon you will come to realize that insights have the power to transform our actions subconsciously. You might still have the same types of problems that you had before, but you will seem to handle them differently now. Every obstacle won't make you feel helpless. Every problem won't seem like a crisis. And everything won't seem to be happening at a fever pitch. As you apply what you have learned from this book, a sense of serenity will descend upon you. You will feel complete and at peace with yourself.

I want to acknowledge you for your willingness to change and to grow. It takes a great deal of courage to take your future into your hands. You should be very proud of yourself for every ounce of effort that you have put forth. And keep in mind that no one is perfect. I don't know anyone who excels at every area covered in this book. I have a long way to go in terms of improving my own character traits and empowering others just like everyone else does. I just try to do the best that I can. I am dedicated to being the best person I can be, but I am also human and fallible. I guess I would rather fail at trying to reach my full potential than to succeed at staying the same.

And to me, the greatest accomplishment one can achieve from reading this book is to make use of the information to become closer to other people. This is not only valuable for being a great catch and for enjoying our lives, but somehow, when we are old and sitting in a rocking chair, I think that we will see our close relationships as the most valuable accomplishments of our lives. So I stand beside you, together, in this great journey of fulfilling our potentials. May it assist you to *become* a great catch, to *marry* a great catch, and to create a healthy, stable relationship that will last a lifetime!

With warm regards,
Hilary Rich

HILARY RICH is the author of *Get Married Now*, the popular book that has helped many people to get married. She has appeared on national television talk shows, and has been on both national and international radio programs. She has been the subject of magazine cover stories and has been featured in newspapers and magazines all across the country. Hilary has lectured to thousands of single people from coast to coast, and hosts the national infomercial called "The Get Married Now Program." She lives with her husband, Steven, a physician, whom she found by using her own Get Married Now™ Plan. They have a two-year-old daughter and another baby on the way!